REAPPORTIONING LEGISLATURES

A Consideration of Criteria and Computers

Edited by

Howard D. Hamilton

Bowling Green State University

CHARLES E. MERRILL BOOKS, INC.,
Columbus, Ohio

Library of Congress Catalog Number: 66-28769

PREFACE

This volume comprises papers presented at a conference, "Representation for Ten Million Ohioans," at Bowling Green State University, March 4-5, 1966. The conference was a colloquium on the theory and practice of representation. Although some papers treat Ohio data and experience, all deal with issues, theories, and problems of a national scope; therefore, the papers are of relevance to all fifty states.

Perceiving the potential nationwide utility of the conference papers, the University authorized publication. The contributors are grateful to Dean Archie Jones of Bowling Green State University for this permission, and to Sandra Weaver and Kay Dauterman, secretaries of the Department of Political Science, who prepared the conference materials and then this manuscript. Credit also is due the 150 political science colleagues who cooperated in the survey reported in Chapter Five, and the Ohio officials, Leagues of Women Voters, and other civic activists who contributed generously to the conference and thereby made this volume possible.

Howard D. Hamilton, ed.

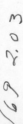

CONTENTS

iv

chapter one

Introduction: The Stage and Cast

This volume begins where most of the literature on apportionment ends. The plethora of literature on this topic has dealt with the controversy over "equal representation," arguing the pros and cons of equally populated districts and rural and urban virtue. Most of the literature has been polemical and ephemeral, documenting the disparities in representation, describing the politics of reapportionment, and reporting the latest incidents in that protracted and intense political struggle, which was triggered by the 1950 census and concluded decisively on June 15, 1964 in the "marble palace," as the Supreme Court embraced the doctrine of equally populated districts for both chambers of legislatures in the *Reynolds* and fourteen companion cases.

In the months subsequent to *Reynolds v. Sims*, the apportionment logjam has dissolved, most of the states have begun to reapportion, and it is evident that the victory of the "one man-one vote" partisans is almost assured. The lingering efforts of their opponents to cancel the Supreme Court's policy by amending the Constitution appear to be futile. Even if by some miracle the "Dirksen amendment" proponents could muster the two-thirds majorities in both chambers of Congress, the proposition would have scant chance of being ratified by three-fourths of the legislatures after they have been reconstituted on a population basis. Time has run out quickly. Thus it follows that most, say 90 per cent, of the reapportionment literature is passé.

1

Introduction: The Stage and Cast

This volume looks forward. The contributors start from the premise that the era of equal representation is an established fact, but their additional premise is that equality of district populations or representation units is not the alpha and omega of fair and good representation.[1] Their view is that the *Reynolds* case is more of a starting than a terminal whistle. The conclusion of the equal representation hassle frees us to rethink the whole gamut of the theory and practice of legislative representation, as officials and citizens in most states proceed with revising their constitutions and reconstructing their assemblies.

Some, indeed many and knowledgeable, people would say that there are only three legitimate criteria for districting, those frequently specified in federal apportionment acts which mandated that congressional districts be "composed of contiguous and compact territory, as nearly equal in population as practicable." Those criteria—the trinity, they say—should be applied resolutely with no regard to other considerations, letting the chips fall where they may. To consider any consequences of the districting, they argue, would be a species of gerrymandering even if not for partisan advantage. That position is logical and reflects integrity, but it also is simplistic.

When one actually puts the pencil to the map, the trinity factors themselves will collide, and one is obliged to make value judgments in striking a balance among population equality and compactness and symmetry. And the aspiring cartographer will soon find himself compelled to weigh other factors. To what extent should population equality be sacrificed in order to follow jurisdictional lines—county, city, township, or ward? Should cities or counties be divided? Such questions lead to that hardy perennial: the relative merits of multi-member and single-member districts.

When the cartographer gets into a metropolis he will be beset by myriad value conflicts. Should Negro areas be lumped into one or few districts where they will predominate, or are Negroes better served by being in several districts which *might* augment their political leverage, although fewer Negroes might be elected? Or should he ignore that category of census data on the theory that designing districts favorable to Negroes (or the poor) is "reverse discrimination"? (Will he be permitted to ignore it?)

---

[1] A careful reader will observe that some contributors are critical of the Supreme Court's treatment of this subject in the *Reynolds* and other cases.

That may lead to the even broader question: Is representative government more fully realized by districts that are homogeneous in socio-economic and ethnic composition, or by heterogeneous districts? The former view is widely held, if not clearly perceived, but a powerful case can be made to the contrary. This may be the most fundamental and baffling issue in districting today. Perhaps this points up the significance, magnitude, and complexity of the task at hand. Representation theory must be reviewed in the light of an urban-industrial society; it was easier for Jefferson and for the drafters of the state constitutions in the age of Jackson.

The issue of homogeneous versus heterogeneous districts leads ineluctably to a related question. Should districting be cognizant of "interests"? And if so, whose interests? Here the hapless cartographer slides into Justice Frankfurter's "quagmire." Perhaps he may wish to retreat, arguing that selection and weighing of interests is so utterly subjective that it should be eschewed. He may add that those people who talk about representing interests and espouse "little federal plans" are only throwing up smoke screens to resist equal representation and to preserve their illegitimate political advantage.

That is a plausible position, but some members of this symposium, even devotees of the "one man-one vote" philosophy, argue that consideration of interests is legitimate and essential. Possibly some blue-ribbon, nonpartisan or unpartisan apportionment agency might district with scant reference to interests, perhaps using a computer with a simple program, but will a legislature?

Several of the contributors assert that apportionment definitely should be cognizant of one category of interests: political parties. Being scholars, they deprecate gerrymandering (and suggest antidotes), but they argue that the impact on parties and elections are fundamental touchstones for appraisal of any districting pattern. Therefore, they raise a host of questions: Does the districting pattern operate neutrally partywise? What is its impact on party cohesion in the assembly? Does it foster or obstruct "party government"? Is it sensitive or insensitive to electoral tides? Is it an instrument of majority or minority rule?

A futuristic touch is furnished by a contributer who is knowledgeable in computerology—a designer of one of the few apportionment programs. What are the various ways of using computers in apportionment? What are the characteristics of the extant programs and is the machine really superior to our mythical cartographer's pencil? Will districting by computer really be universal by 1980?

The participants make no claim to an exhaustive canvassing of all the factors pertinent to legislative representation, nor do they offer a definitive list of criteria. Perhaps they raise more questions than they answer. If so, that is confirmation of how much is unknown about representation and the need for more investigation and more discussion.

Each participant has engaged in research on facets of representation, either in ivy halls or as attorneys in reapportionment litigation. Perhaps a brief statement of their credentials is in order. If the stage has been set, the cast will be introduced in the order of entrances:

James K. Pollock, Murfin professor at the University of Michigan and authority on both American and German government, has been studying electoral-representation systems on both sides of the Atlantic for many years. He was chairman of the committee on apportionment at the Michigan constitutional convention of 1962.

Malcolm Jewell of the University of Kentucky is a student of legislative politics, the author of two textbooks and numerous journal articles, and editor of a volume on *The Politics of Reapportionment*.

William Saxbe has been attorney general of Ohio for six years, following several years as a leader of the Ohio house of representatives. As attorney for state officials in reapportionment litigation, including two trips to the Supreme Court, he has had occasion to become informed of the legal criteria.

Byron Marlowe teaches political science at Bowling Green University and currently is engaged in research on apportionment criteria.

Stuart Jaffy, a practicing attorney, also acquired his knowledge in this area by being a counselor in the Ohio reapportionment cases.

Thomas Flinn of Oberlin College has labored assiduously in state politics, attested by a stream of journal articles.

Howard Hamilton of Bowling Green University has been engaged in research on aspects of representation, reflected in numerous articles and one book. He also has drafted some apportionment bills and otherwise participated in reapportionment in three states.

Myron Q. Hale teaches American government and politics at the Ohio State University. His graduate seminar on legislative politics has produced two monographs on representation and a computer program for districting.

William P. Irwin, chairman of political science at Western Reserve University, was a co-author of Professor Jewell's book and presently is doing research with him on the characteristics of multi-member districts.

chapter two

Reapportionment and
Fair Representation

James K. Pollock

Since the decision of the United States Supreme Court in the case of *Baker v. Carr* in 1962, the whole country has been concerned with the problem of apportionment. A mild revolution in political relationships has already occurred following the later decision in *Reynolds v. Sims* which decreed that *both* houses of a state legislature must be apportioned on the basis of population. "One man-one vote"—the effective propaganda slogan of the proponents of reapportionment, was now adopted by the Supreme Court as the law of the land.

Legislatures all over the land were ordered by courts—both state and federal—sometimes by both—to comply with the U.S. Supreme Court's general prescription of equal population as a basis for all apportionments. In some cases changes were accomplished without too much delay or difficulty; in others, interminable and even incredible actions were taken which have confused the public and which in some cases have not yet brought solutions. In New York, state courts were pitted against federal courts; in Michigan, the State Supreme Court, having decreed a new apportionment, a year later ordered its reconsideration; in Colorado the vote of the people was voided. And the end is not yet! What is happening today to state legislatures will happen tomorrow to county boards of supervisors and to city councils.

6

But nothing is gained now by complaining about what has been done. Justice Frankfurter was right, in the opinion of the author, when he urged the court to keep out of this "political thicket," and Justice Harlan was irrefutable when he wrote that the Fourteenth Amendment never was intended to have anything to do with apportionment. But they were overruled, and some kind of an egalitarian revolt seems to exist, dictated by the courts.

In this situation it behooves political scientists, civic leaders, and legislators to think through the whole process of representation, since the courts, with few exceptions, have failed to do so. Political scientists must shoulder some of the blame for the present simplistic solution of the very complicated apportionment problem. Despite several limited studies in a few states, political scientists have not conducted much research in depth into the effect of differing apportionment formulas. The great complexity of the subject was little realized. Politicians and legislators had played around with the subject for decades, and the place of apportionment in the total election picture and its relationship to representative government had been discussed by a few theorists, but not subjected to thoroughgoing empirical research. As is so frequently the case in politics, pat formulas and political polemics took the front of the stage.

Now the pieces must be pulled together. As Professor Alfred de Grazia so well puts it, "apportionment is part of the system of elections in a representative government." What is reflected in an apportionment? Must apportionments be drawn in terms of any one theory of representation such as strict population, community or neighborhood groupings, economic or regional similarities, political or historical traditions? What has the study of group dynamics revealed about the problem of apportionment? Should "a heavy-handed application of sixth grade arithmetics," as Justice Stewart characterized the majority decision in the Reynolds case, prevail or is not fair representation the primary concern? Chief Justice Warren at one point in his opinion said, "the achieving of fair and effective representation for all citizens is concededly the basic aim of legislative apportionment," but the Reynolds decision did not give full effect to this sound goal.

---

[1]Alfred de Grazia, *Apportionment and Representative Government* (New York: Frederick A. Praeger, Inc. 1963), p. 18.

There should still be time for reason to prevail and for fair representative systems to be established, and with this purpose in mind the author proposes to suggest certain aspects of the apportionment problem which need attention. For the purposes of this discussion the problem of reapportionment will be divided into two levels: one, the process or mechanics of reapportionment, and two, the philosophy of representation which an apportionment system attempts to carry out.

First, consider the machinery of government for districting. It has been deplorable. It was the almost complete breakdown of this machinery which brought about the present situation. If the states had followed their own constitutions, if state legislatures had done what they were supposed to do in the matter of reapportionment, there would not have been the violent public reaction and the precipitate intervention of the courts. Thus it seems fair to say that something drastic needs to be done in the various states to give assurance of the enactment in the future of whatever systems of apportionment are considered legal and constitutional.

The best discussion of this subject is to be found in the recent report of the Advisory Commission on Intergovernmental Relations.[2] Their guidelines shall be adopted for purposes of this discussion. It is significant that the members of this Commission representing all levels of government were unanimous in making these recommendations regarding procedures to be followed by the states, even though they disagreed on other matters.

First of all, the Commission pointed out that apportionment of seats in state legislative bodies is a basic factor of representative government, and provisions relating thereto should be clearly specified in state constitutions. Second, the apportionment formula for each body of the state legislature should be spelled out in clear and sufficient detail so that there can be no question as to the meaning of the formula. Third, the state constitution should specify the frequency of state reapportionment. Fourth, the state constitution should specify the body or officer having a responsibility for apportioning seats in the state legislature. Fifth, the Commission recommended that state courts be constitutionally provided with appropriate jurisdiction and remedies to ensure that state officials

---

[2]*Apportionment of State Legislatives,* Report of the Advisory Commission on Intergovernmental Relations, December, 1962, pp. 59-66.

comply with their apportionment responsibility. And finally, the Commission recommended that the actual apportionment of a state legislature, including as it must many elements of negotiation and accommodation that do not lend themselves to adversary proceedings, should be accomplished by the legislative or other specified non-judicial body or officer. The Commission believes that state and federal courts should confine their role to insuring that non-judicial body or officer promptly produce a reasonable apportionment meeting constitutional requirements and urges both state and federal courts to avoid, except in the most extreme circumstances, the prescription by judicial decree of specific apportionment formulas or the geographic composition of legislative districts.

It will be recognized that all of these recommendations, although dealing with very controversial matters, are based upon the hard and frequently unfortunate experience which the various states have had in dealing with reapportionment. All of these recommendations not only are soundly based on experience, but have the recommendation of a highly respected Commission representing all levels of government as well as legislative and executive branches of national, state and local governments.

Having worked on this problem as a delegate in the recent Michigan Constitutional Convention, having watched the Apportionment Commission, and having observed the actions of the Courts, this writer admits to a certain disillusionment, or even cynicism, with regard to any procedures which are decided upon. But in any case, having thought the matter through not merely as an arm-chair philosopher but as a practitioner, this writer believes that the most satisfactory and effective way of securing regular apportionment—bearing in mind the recommendations already presented—is to give the job to the chief election officer in the state who is usually the Secretary of State, and thus to remove apportionment from state legislatures or other special bodies. If a clear and rational formula can be specified in the Constitution, then the chief election officer has only the administrative job of giving effect to the constitutional mandate, subject, of course, always to court mandamus and court review.

Why has the problem of reapportionment not been placed in the hands of administrative officers, who could be experts in these matters? In Britain such matters are handled by Boundary Commissions consisting principally of civil servants, and the parties have always accepted the results.[3] Also in Western Germany, which recently underwent a redistricting, the Reapportionment Commission, consisting also of civil servants, accomplished their task and received the approbation of all parties and the approval of Parliament.[4] In the German case, it is interesting to point out, the Commission even prepared a table which showed whatever slight advantages there were to all parties in the results which they had drawn up.

So much for the machinery and procedures of reapportionment. Now to be discussed is the basis of reapportionment and the political values and philosophy which must necessarily be considered in deciding on a proper formula. Students and practitioners concerned with apportionment must have an awareness of the great complexity of the total political process; they must also be conscious of the theories and problems of effective representation, and be cognizant of what has come to be called group dynamics. As Professor Robert Dixon has said: "Reapportionment and redistricting involve representation, and representation is the political heart of any democratic system. It is important to understand exactly *what* is to be represented in a legislative body and *how.* Fair representation as it has been understood down through the centuries obviously involves population as a basic factor, but to base apportionment merely on faceless numbers is to lose sight of the controlling influences in contemporary society.

Hence, treating people as fungible and overlooking everything else involved in fair representation is to take a very narrow view. Reference is made to such factors as compactness, contiguity following county, township, and city lines, minority representation, single-member versus multi-member districts, etc.

In considering all of these factors one obviously has a number of choices, bearing in mind that every line drawn on a map makes one or more policy choices. What seems to have been so egregiously overlooked in many of the current apportionments, is that well-established communities should not be unduly broken up and that mere arithmetic is not the only important thing. Or as Justice

---

[3]David Butler, "The Redistribution of Seats," *Public Administration,* Summer, 1955, pp. 125-147.
[4]James K. Pollock, "A Sensible Approach," *National Civic Review,* LIV, No. 7, (July, 1965), 357-361.
[5]Paper presented in Washington, Oct. 22, 1965, p. 3.

Harlan put it in the Reynolds case, "people are not ciphers and legislators can represent their electors only by speaking for their interests—many of which do reflect the place where the electors live." In the opinion of Chief Justice Warren in the same case, "a state may legitimately desire to maintain the integrity of various political subdivisions, insofar as possible . . . valid considerations may underline such aims." And he continued, "So long as the divergencies from a strict population standard are based on legitimate considerations incident to the effectuation of a rational state policy, some deviations from the equal population principle are constitutionally permissible . . . in either or both houses. . . ." Professor Dixon has effectively stated the problem in these words: "When we apportion and district, and set up a multi-membered, deliberative body, should not our goal be fair and effective representation, and responsiveness to the group dynamics of American politics? And if so, isn't this something different, something much more complex and interesting than is connoted by the phrase one man-one vote?"[6]

If one man-one vote is taken literally as the state Supreme Court did in Michigan, then the more equal the districts the better, with a variation range of around two per cent—many within one-half of one per cent—all under a census five years old. But the result is frequently to ignore political subdivision lines and to create a number of gerrymandered districts. The Michigan Supreme Court, ignoring the carefully drafted provisions of the new Constitution which were intended to prevent gerrymandering, is now considering other plans which more closely follow county and other subdivision lines, and which would avoid dividing Republican and Negro areas for political purposes. The point to be emphasized here is that factors other than population deserve careful consideration and attention, and to permit reasonable population deviations, perhaps of five or ten per cent, is to recognize community and other factors, and to avoid unfair representation of areas and groups. After much reflection, the author believes that the Michigan formula of 80-20 for the Senate would have achieved fair representation, but it was summarily declared *unconstitutional* and voided.

---

[6]Paper read at The Midwest Conference of Political Scientists, Indiana University, April 22, 1965.

Again, quoting Professor Dixon, who has carefully thought this problem through, "The numbers game is not very meaningful when one uses only the Dauer-Kelsay scale and the population variance ratio. The latter compares only the one largest and the one smallest district, and ignores the more meaningful concept of average deviation. The former, the Dauer-Kelsay scale figure of the minimum population which theoretically could control a majority of seats, not only ignores but flies in the face of actual voting behavior. And even taking it at face value, it must be noted that in a sizable legislature an allowable maximum deviation of 15 per cent will yield a scale figure of under 44 per cent and a deviation of 25 per cent will yield a figure of under 38 per cent."[7]

But quite as important is that consideration be given to minority representation. Implicit in the single-member district system is the fact that the party that wins the district, however closely, gets all the representation, and the only corrective in a state legislature for this possible arbitrariness is that over the state as a whole the minority is able to level out its representation and thus end up with reasonable overall representation. This is much more important than how much one district deviates from another. Various scales which have been devised, illuminate some inequities, but they do not help very much in arriving at fair representation, including minority representation.

Out of the present apportionment quagmire may come a wider discussion of the feasibility of proportional representation in choosing genuinely representative assemblies. It is an interesting story why proportional representation has not caught on in the United States. It has been called un-American and unconstitutional; it has been tied too much to the single transferable vote system, and it has always been dubbed as "foreign." Nevertheless, a proper list system, with a single choice within the list, not only would be an easy system to administer, but would result in fairer representation.

Perhaps even the U.S. Supreme Court may be receptive to factors other than population. In the recent case of *Fortson v. Dorsey*, the Supreme Court in a dictum rather than a decision seemed to take a long step away from its previous narrow mathe-

---

[7] *Ibid.*, p. 12. See also 63 *Michigan Law Review* (1964) 209.

matical approach. Speaking through Mr. Justice Brennan the Court said "it might well be that, designedly or otherwise, a multi-member constituency apportionment scheme, under the circumstances of a particular case, would operate to minimize or cancel out the voting strength of racial or political elements of the voting population. When this is demonstrated it will be time enough to consider whether the system still passes constitutional muster."

One final point. Since the Supreme Court has applied mathematical equality to *both* houses of a state legislature, the need for having two houses at all may be questioned. Justice Warren took some pains to discuss this point in the Reynolds case, but it seems that he was quite unconvincing. If the basis of representation in two houses is to be the same, there is another reason, in addition to those formerly presented, to argue for unicameralism. Nebraska, the Canadian provinces, and all the West German states except Bavaria, manage to struggle along without the expense and lack of responsibility of the bicameral system. At any rate, students and civic leaders should give renewed attention to the desirability of a unicameral legislature.

In conclusion, as Chief Justice Warren said, "The achieving of fair and effective representation for all citizens is concededly the basic aim of legislative apportionment." If the numbers game could be avoided and the total election process explored in order to understand the real nature of individual and interest representation, the solution to the apportionment problem would be moving in the proper direction. To continue to treat people as just a collection of "faceless census statistics," as Professor Dixon puts it, is a very naïve understanding of majority rule. Political scientists must recognize, as Professor Dixon has so well stated,[7] "one man-one vote, translated simply as equal population districts, and applied thus to problems of representation in a mass democracy, is a sterile concept, and fails to provide a workable premise."[8] More than numbers are involved. Even computers will not solve the problem although they might help in its solution. Although much damage will probably be done by past carelessness and negligence, there is no reason why political scientists cannot get ready for the next big round of apportionments which will follow the 1970 census.

---

[8]*Ibid.*, p. 21.

chapter three

Criteria Reflected in Recent Apportionments

Malcolm E. Jewell

The apportionments that have recently been enacted by state legislatures across the country do not constitute a single clear pattern, but it is possible to define certain principles of apportionment that are becoming widely accepted and to delineate the areas of uncertainty and controversy that remain. It is not possible to make a sharp distinction between legislative and judicial standards, because, ever since the decision in *Baker v. Carr*, legislative discretion in apportionment has been limited by judicially imposed requirements.

Because the Supreme Court did not provide any specific standards for apportionment in its 1962 *Baker* decision and because subsequent lower court decisions were often contradictory, many state legislatures initially passed reapportionment laws that gave only slightly greater weight to the population factor, and some of the new apportionments made one house less representative of population while making the other house more representative. The decisions of the Supreme Court in June, 1964, in *Reynolds v. Sims* and related cases brought an end to the judicial confusion and made it clear that apportionment in both houses of the legislature must be based primarily on population. The legislatures had lost their excuse for temporizing, and for the first time most

14

of them began to grapple seriously with the problem of devising apportionments based as nearly as practicable on the principle of equal population. At the time of the *Reynolds* decision there were only five states in which the apportionment appeared to conform to judicial standards. In the next eighteen months thirty-four states adopted apportionment plans, or had them imposed by the courts, which were based more nearly on population. Ten other states were under court order to act or were facing court suits. Not all of the apportionments enacted after the *Reynolds* decision were accepted by the courts, but gradually the gap between judicial expectation and legislative performance was being closed. In at least two states, Indiana and New York, the legislature passed several plans at one time and left it to the court to decide which of the plans met judicial standards.

At the same time that state legislatures were taking steps to conform to the *Reynolds* decision, more than half of the legislatures were petitioning Congress to adopt a constitutional amendment that would permit factors other than population to be taken into account in apportioning legislatures. But the campaign for this amendment faltered in the states, while the amendment, proposed by Senator Everett Dirksen, twice was debated by the United States Senate and twice failed to win the necessary two-thirds vote. The failure of the drive for constitutional change has probably stirred the legislatures into more rapid compliance with the equal population principle in apportionment.

Population Standards

The Supreme Court has refused to set any mathematical limits on the variations from equality that may be permitted in the population of districts, although some lower courts have used mathematical standards in judging apportionment plans. These courts have sometimes referred to the minimum percentage of voters that could theoretically elect a legislative majority or to the average deviation in the size of districts, but the standard most frequently used is the maximum deviation. The figure most often cited by the courts as a standard is a 15 per cent deviation above or below the perfect size district. The 15 per cent maximum deviation has been accepted by many state legislatures either as an absolute limit or as a standard with only a few exceptions, but it is by no means universally applicable to the realities of legislative apportionment. Geographical factors and the rigidity of county boundary lines have led some legislative bodies to exceed this limit. Kentucky, for example, was one of the first states after the *Baker* decision to reapportion primarily on the basis of population equality, and the law has not been challenged in the courts. But the presence of 120 counties and 100 single-member House districts guarantees deviations in excess of 15 per cent. There are several counties in that state that would be at least 25 per cent below average if they had two representatives and at least 25 per cent above average if they had only one member. In Wyoming, with its many sparsely populated counties, an apportionment put into effect by court order had variations up to 33 per cent.

County Boundaries

Most state legislatures have preferred to accept larger variations in the size of districts rather than to break up counties into pieces in the formation of districts. The Supreme Court has made it clear that the goal of population equality does not require that county lines be ignored. The main argument for retaining county lines is that in most states the county is a significant political unit with a community of interests and often a degree of socio-economic homogeneity. In some states local legislation is extensively used, and for this reason the county deserves representation. An additional reason for maintaining county boundaries is that these help to minimize gerrymandering. As the Supreme Court has said, indiscriminate districting without regard to county lines is an "invitation to gerrymandering."

Nevertheless, a few apportionments have been enacted that did not use county or city lines as the basis for district boundaries. Such laws in both New York and Michigan were accepted by the courts, at least as temporary expedients. These examples illustrate the risks of ignoring existing political subdivisions. In both cases one political party was responsible for the districting plans and the other party raised loud cries of gerrymandering. The judicial requirement for periodic and equitable apportionment increases the temptation to engage in gerrymandering, and the retention of county boundaries—which has been the practice in most state legislatures—is probably the best available method of discouraging at least the most blatant forms of gerrymandering.

Districting in Metropolitan Counties

As an increasing proportion of legislators are elected from metropolitan counties, the problem of districting within these multi-member counties is receiving greater attention. In some states there are few precedents to rely on because metropolitan counties in the past have not had more than one member in one house of the legislature. There are three methods of districting that have been extensively used in metropolitan counties: single-member districts; several multi-member districts, each electing a small number of members; and one multi-member district in which all of the county's legislators are chosen at large. In either kind of multi-member district there are two ways in which the legislators may be elected. One is the "place" method, which requires that each candidate designate for which place or position he is running; the other might be called the "free for all" method, which requires that all of the candidates run against each other. Prior to the *Baker* decision in 1962 approximately two-thirds of all senators elected in multi-member counties were chosen in single-member districts and the remainder were elected county-wide. In the lower house of state legislatures slightly more than one-third of the members from multi-member counties were chosen by each of these methods, and the remainder were selected in counties that were divided into several multi-member districts.

The question of districting within metropolitan counties is probably the most important remaining unsolved problem of legislative apportionment. It is important because the method of districting affects the representation of political parties and other interests within the metropolitan counties. The effects of districting on political party representation are relatively easy to measure, but the effects on racial, ethnic, economic, and other interest groups may be just as important though less susceptible to precise measurement. Proportional representation is the only technique that is designed to represent all political parties in proportion to their voting strength, but the lower house in Illinois, which has a cumulative voting system in three-man districts, is the only state legislative body using any form of proportional representation. Any other districting scheme wastes the votes of the minority party. In a county-wide at-large election it is common for a slate of candidates from one party to be elected, leaving unrepresented the minority-party voters, who might easily constitute 40 or 45 per cent of the electorate. In a single-member district plan, the majority party is likely to elect more members than would be indicated by its proportion of the electorate, but the minority party usually has pockets of strength within the county that enables it to elect some members. The partisan effects of a single-member district plan depend on the way in which district lines have been drawn. The majority party in the legislature may engage in a gerrymandering operation that wastes the votes of the minority party in a county either by splitting up the minority voters among a number of districts or by concentrating them in one or a few districts in order to safeguard the remainder for the majority party.

In most metropolitan counties there are other interests that can be located geographically. Negroes and other ethnic minorities are often concentrated in the center of the city; and suburbanites often share common interests and needs. An at-large method of electing legislators reduces the possibility of giving representation to each of the major interests in a metropolitan area, although it is always possible that in a primary or general election a slate of candidates will be formed that represents a variety of these interests. Although various interests have a stake in the choice of a districting method, the racial implications of metropolitan districting have been emphasized most often in recent controversies, particularly those that have arisen in the South.

The districting methods used in metropolitan counties have other implications. In a county electing many legislators, the at-large method imposes a difficult burden on the voter, particularly in primary elections. In a county selecting ten to fifteen members he may have to choose from among as many as forty or fifty candidates in the primary. One of the consequences may be that the voters are forced to rely more heavily on endorsements made by party organizations or other groups. Candidates running at large in either the primary or the general election in a large county may have to rely more heavily on organizational assistance and financial support from party or interest groups than they would in single-member districts. On the other hand, the division of a large county into single-member districts necessitates the revision of boundaries every decade, with each revision offering opportunities for gerrymandering, while population shifts within the counties may create serious inequalities among the districts before the decade is over and it is time to redistrict.

In several two-party states that have used multi-member districts in the past, there has been a trend toward single-member districts, although in some cases the evidence comes from interim apportionments rather than from permanent changes in the constitution. Pennsylvania, Ohio, and Colorado are states in which temporary districting plans endorsed by the courts included single-member districts for metropolitan counties. Ohio and Colorado had previously used at-large districts for these counties, and Pennsylvania had used several multi-member districts per county. The new Michigan constitution now in effect substitutes single-member for small multi-member districts (of two or three members) in metropolitan counties.

The question of legislative districting is more acute in the South, because in the past southern metropolitan counties have rarely been divided into legislative districts. Most of these counties have had only a single senator, and in the lower house only the metropolitan counties in Kentucky and Orleans parish in Louisiana used single-member districts prior to the *Baker* decision. Several southern states, including Alabama, Florida, Virginia, and North Carolina, have continued the practice of electing all members in metropolitan counties at large. Texas divided the largest county, Harris, into three multi-member districts, but continued at-large elections for House members in the remaining metropolitan counties. In its most recent reapportionment Tennessee divided the five largest counties into single-member Senate and House districts. Georgia has developed a complicated combination of districting methods for its largest counties. Senators are elected from single-member districts. In the House most of the large counties elect several representatives at large, and in addition these counties are divided into districts from each of which a number of members—ranging from one to four—are elected.

A number of factors have influenced legislative decisions on districting across the country. Often one of the political parties anticipates that it will benefit from changing the method of districting. Negro groups have usually advocated single-member districts, and southern advocates of at-large elections have frequently emphasized that this method would minimize the chance of Negro legislators being elected. In Florida the conflict over districting in Dade County (Miami) is closely related to controversies over metropolitan government; those who want to weaken the strong consolidated county government have been advocating single-member districts. In many states support for dividing metropolitan counties into legislative districts comes from rural legislators who believe that this technique is most likely to prevent bloc voting by metropolitan legislators and thereby will weaken urban power in the legislature.

The controversy over districting is not limited to metropolitan counties. In some states multi-county, multi-member districts are used to assure greater equality of representation without violating county boundaries. Thus three counties, each of which has two-thirds of the population necessary to elect a member, may be joined to elect two members. Where counties of grossly unequal size are joined in a multi-member district, however, the effect may be to minimize the smaller county's chance to elect one of its own citizens to the legislature, and such districting patterns have encountered judicial disapproval. In Florida a huge multi-county district electing several senators at large has been created in the northen part of the state, apparently as a device for safeguarding several veteran senators from that area. In Alabama the court disapproved several multi-member, multi-county districts, on the grounds that they were designed to submerge counties with a Negro majority in districts with a white majority.

Although some courts have criticized the combination of single- and multi-member districts in one house, most state legislatures remain free to choose among various methods of districting. The best clue to judicial attitudes in the future was the warning by the Supreme Court, in a Georgia case, that multi-member districts might "operate to minimize or cancel out the voting strength of racial or political elements of the voting population" and, if so, might be subject to judicial scrutiny. However, in its subsequent review of apportionment in Hawaii, the Court emphasized that it could not assume that multi-member districts would have such a discriminatory effect in the absence of evidence, which it found lacking in the Hawaiian apportionment case.

State Constitutions

In many states the constitutional provisions on apportionment have been overruled or modified by judicial action because they violated the principle of one man-one vote. In the absence of valid constitutional requirements, state legislatures have been free to enact any apportionment that would satisfy the courts. Once the problems of legislative action have been solved, the states will be turning increasingly to the problems of constitutional revision. New constitutional provisions, of course, must meet the judicial standards of one man-one vote, but in some states it is possible that the voters will reject the formulas for apportionment that are acceptable to the courts. In the past, for example, California voters have rejected plans to give the metropolitan counties a much more modest increase in representation than has now been enacted by the legislature under pressure from the courts. In September, 1965, the voters in Texas rejected a constitutional amendment that would have increased the size of the Senate and permitted the largest counties to have more than a single senator. The courts can overrule constitutional amendments adopted by popular vote, as the Supreme Court did in the case of Colorado, but they cannot force the voters to approve an apportionment amendment based on population.

In some states the voters have approved amendments to incorporate the one man-one vote principle in the constitution. The Connecticut voters accepted such a plan in December, 1965. The voters in Mississippi rejected a constitutional amendment that gave an advantage to rural counties and subsequently accepted an apportionment plan based more nearly on population. In most of the states in which the apportionment provisions of the constitution are invalid, the tasks of drafting new provisions and winning voter approval for them remain to be accomplished.

One feature that is likely to be adopted as a part of the constitutional requirements for apportionment in some states is the use of a board or commission to carry out the apportionment in one or both houses, either on its own initiative or following the failure of the legislature to act within a prescribed time period after the decennial census. Before the *Baker* decision, six states delegated the authority to reapportion one or both houses to such a board, and six others gave a board the responsibility for acting when the legislature failed to do so. In the past there has been no guarantee that a board would be any more successful than the legislature. Although its members did not have a personal stake in preserving the status quo, they were often subject to the same political motivations as legislatures. It was the failure of both the legislature and a board to take action in Illinois that led to the selection of the lower house in at-large elections in 1964.

In January, 1966, the voters in Missouri voted to use a commission to apportion the House, such as had been used for a number of years in apportioning the Senate. It is too early to tell whether there is any trend toward greater reliance on boards or commissions. They are likely to be relied on more heavily in those states where the constitutional standards for apportionment leave little room for discretion. For example, if there are a large enough number of legislative seats compared to the number of counties so that nearly every county is assured at least one seat, the apportioning of seats to counties becomes a simple question of mathematics. However, the creation of multi-county districts and of districts within the larger counties has implications both for the political parties and for the incumbent legislators that may inspire the legislature to retain, if possible, its authority over the apportionment and districting processes.

Conclusion

The questions about the apportionment process that remain unanswered do not concern the principle of equal population or even the range of variation that should be permitted in applying this principle. Since the *Reynolds* decision in 1964 the state legislatures have been gradually incorporating this principle into apportionment laws under the watchful eyes of the courts. The unanswered questions involve districting, and particularly the use of districts within metropolitan counties. The state legislatures have devised, and the courts have generally tolerated, a variety of solutions to the problem of giving the various partisan and other interests with the metropolis an equitable voice in the legislature. For the most part the legislatures have given more attention to protecting partisan interests and incumbent legislators than to achieving an ideal balance of interests in the representative process.

It is obvious from the poll presented in another chapter that political scientists are far from unanimous in their views on the criteria for districting. Until we know more about the realities of the representative process, particularly in metropolitan areas, political scientists will be ill-equipped to give advice or to complain about the motivations of legislators. The judicial mandate to reapportion offers the legislators a chance to experiment with a variety of districting techniques, perhaps even to try a proportional representation plan like the Illinois cumulative voting plan. Bicameralism makes it possible to use contrasting techniques in the two houses. Perhaps political scientists should encourage legislators to experiment with any plan that is based on the equal population principle and avoids blatant discrimination against racial or partisan groups.

chapter four

Criteria Established by Court Decisions

William B. Saxbe

When the Ohio Legislature adjourned without acting on apportionment, it became apparent that some further action would have to be taken. The federal court, under its mandate from the Supreme Court, would not allow the 1966 elections to be held under the existing plan. That meant that a new apportionment would have to be devised.

It was necessary, therefore, to ascertain the guidelines that would govern any new apportionment. All of the federal and state court cases were studied, and from them ground rules were distilled. By late summer, 1965, there were enough cases that one could perceive the characteristics of a safe plan and also pitfalls which were likely to lead to constitutional difficulties. It was decided that any plan would have to meet the federal constitutional guidelines which will be discussed below.

Since the fall of 1965, there have been a number of additional court opinions, dealing with many of the different problems that arise in reapportionment. Not all of these cases are consistent with one another; some have been appealed. By and large they bear out our original conclusions held by the Ohio legislature. There has been no case which has held or indicated that the ground rules are inconsistent with the federal guidelines. Some cases have been a little more liberal, that is, they have allowed a little less equality, but it is clear from every court decision in the country that if these ground rules are followed, an apportionment will be acceptable, insofar as the federal constitution is concerned.

Equality of Representation

The weight of each vote for members of both houses of a bicameral legislature must be approximately equal to the weight of every other vote.

Whether legislators represent approximately an equal number of voters can be determined by dividing the population of the state by the total number of representatives, and considering the quotient as the population which, ideally, each legislator should represent. The district of any given legislator is then compared to this perfect district. For example, if the population of the state is 10 million, and the number of representatives is 100, the perfect district has 100,000 inhabitants. A district of 115,000 inhabitants has a population 15 per cent above that of the perfect district.

The deviation between districts is sometimes expressed as a ratio of the population of the largest district to that of the smallest district. For example, a plan which has one district with a population of 15 per cent above that of the perfect district, and another 15 per cent below that of the perfect district, has a population variance ratio of 1.35 to 1; or in other words the largest district is 1.35 times the population of the smallest district.

The Supreme Court has refused to set a mathematical standard which an apportionment system must meet. It said that "both houses of a state legislature must be apportioned on a population basis" and "a state must make an honest and good faith effort to construct districts, in both houses of its legislature, as nearly of equal population as is practicable." *Reynolds v. Sims.* It did say, in *Lucas v. 44th General Assembly of Colorado* that a plan with a population variance ratio of 1.7 to 1 was "at least arguably" permissible, although it reversed a decision upholding the plan.

Most federal district and state supreme courts have assumed that a plan in which no district has a population of more than 15 per cent above or below that of the perfect district is sufficiently equal in population. As the federal district court in Georgia *(Toombs v. Fortson)* said, "a variance of more than 15 per cent would be difficult, if not impossible to justify." Many district courts have not verbally established an allowable percentage deviation, but when the approved and disapproved plans are examined, it is apparent that they followed the 15 per cent rule rather closely.

Some courts have allowed a slightly higher variance for an interim plan, but indicated that such inequality would not be permitted on a permanent basis. Thus the Supreme Court of New Jersey allowed a variance of 27.3 per cent in one district in a plan which is approved as an interim measure only. *Jackman v. Bodine,* and a federal court in Utah allowed a variance ratio of 1.74 to 1 as an interim plan. *(Petuskey v. Rampton).*

A few courts allowed a variance of more than 15 per cent for a district in one house of the legislature, when that variance compensated for an opposite variance for the district in the other house. To illustrate, assume that a county, on a population basis, is entitled to three and three-fourths House members, and one and one-fourth Senators, but is given four House members and one Senator. A few courts approved such inequalities because the under-representation to the district in the one house is compensated by some over-representation in the other house. This reasoning was followed by a federal court in Tennessee *(Baker v. Carr)* and by the federal court in Vermont *(Buckley v. Hoff).* As the Supreme Court said in *Reynolds v. Sims,* "apportionment in one house could be arranged so as to balance off minor inequalities in the representation of certain areas in the other house." However, the word that should be stressed here is *"minor."* The courts will not permit a pattern of discrimination in the Senate, and a pattern of counter-discrimination in the House, and then rule that representation is equal because they balance out. This rule of compensation is a savings clause, not a foundation on which a plan can be erected.

Absent this compensating factor, few cases approved a variance of more than 15 per cent on a permanent basis. One district court in Alabama did indicate that it would approve a plan with a variance of more than 15 per cent, and a district court in Wyoming approved a plan with a variance ratio of more than 2 to 1, but that case is now on appeal to the United States Supreme Court *(Shaefer v. Thompson).*

Another fact that should be mentioned about the equal representation problem is that it cannot be solved in terms of balancing urban versus rural interests. When people first began to discuss reapportionment, it was often mentioned in terms of breaking the so-called "strangle-hold" that the rural interests had on many legislatures, and of giving the urban areas power commensurate with their population. However, the court cases make it clear that a proper balancing of urban and rural interests does not necessarily result in equal representation.

For example, a proper balance of urban and rural interests can exist, although some districts are greatly over-represented and others greatly under-represented. So long as the same proportion of urban and rural districts are over- or under-represented, there will be a proper balancing of urban and rural interests, although there will not be equal representation. Federal district courts in Minnesota *(Honsey v. Donovan)* and Georgia *(Toombs v. Fortson)*, as well as the Pennsylvania Supreme Court *(Butcher v. Bloom)* rejected the urban-rural criteria, and insisted upon equal representation across the state. As the New York District Court said in *WMCA v. Lomenzo*, "*Reynolds v. Sims* is concerned with arithmetic and not geometry." Of course, if there is equal representation, there will be a proper balancing of urban and rural interests. But if there is proper balancing without equal representation, the plan will still be held unconstitutional.

In summary, if districts are created in such a way that each legislator represents, within 15 per cent, the number of people in the perfect district, the mathematical tests will have been met. If under-representation in one House is compensated by over-representation in another, the plan might be acceptable but any deviation of more than that 15 per cent will probably result in the plan being held invalid.

Racial Discrimination

An apportionment plan cannot be used for purposes of racial discrimination.

It is clear that any apportionment plan which is created with the design of discriminating against racial or ethnic groups will violate the equal protection clause of the United States Constitution. Such discrimination can result from the drawing of lines which disfranchise minorities by dividing them among many districts, or by creating multiple-member districts, where minorities are overwhelmed in the monolithic tide of majority ballots.

An original case involving racial discrimination in drawing boundaries was *Gomillion v. Lightfoot*. In that case Alabama had changed the boundaries of the city of Tuskegee so that of the 400 Negroes originally living in the city, only five remained within the boundaries after the change, although not one white voter was eliminated. The Supreme Court held such action violated the equal protection clause of the Fourteenth Amendment.

In *Fortson v. Dorsey* the Supreme Court indicated that it was prepared to carry this doctrine further. It said that it might be that an apportionment plan using multiple-member constituencies would "designedly or otherwise" minimize or cancel out the voting strength of racial elements. Note that the court would question a plan which had such a result, even though the plan had not intended to minimize minority strength.

Thus the court may be prepared to go further than it did in its 1964 opinion in *Wright v. Rockefeller*. That case was concerned with congressional districting. The claim was made that the boundaries of the 17th and 18th New York congressional districts were drawn along racial lines. Negroes comprised 5.1 per cent of the population in the 17th District, compared to 86.3 per cent in the adjacent 18th District. Between the two districts was an eleven-sided, step-shaped boundary, which plaintiff charged was drawn for racial reasons.

The trial court held that this line could be explained by a desire to maintain neighborhood communities and said plaintiff had failed to prove discrimination. The Supreme Court affirmed this holding on the basis of plaintiff's burden of proof. However, in *Wright* it should be noted that the Negroes were represented. They were not overwhelmed by large districts with white populations, nor were they divided among many white districts so that their voice was diluted.

Another case in which plaintiffs sought to raise the racial discrimination issue was *Mann v. Davis*, arising in Virginia. In that case, Henrico County and the City of Richmond has been combined to form one house district, electing eight delegates at large.

Plaintiffs claimed that the city and county should be separated, and that they should be further subdistricted into single-member districts, in order to give the Negroes a chance to elect some representatives. The city of Richmond had approximately 127,000 white residents, and 97,000 non-white, while Henrico County had 111,000 white and 6,000 non-white residents. Plaintiffs claimed the counties were combined to counterbalance the large non-white vote in Richmond, and further, that subdistricting would assure some Negro delegates. The court rejected this contention and approved this part of the plan as drawn.

The district court held that the city and county were combined because, separately, each had population in excess of full ratios, but when combined, their total population equaled approximately eight full ratios and thus it was fair to give them eight delegates. The court further said that no city in Virginia had ever been subdistricted, even for council races, and that equal protection did not require that districts be drawn to assure political success to any one race. This decision was affirmed by the Supreme Court, without opinion.

On the other hand, a federal district court in Texas had ruled that the constitution did not require subdistricting multiple-member counties in order to give Negroes a better chance of election. The case was appealed to the Supreme Court, but before decision, the apportionment act in question was repealed. The Supreme Court thereupon vacated the judgment of the district court. It is interesting to note that the high court did not dismiss the appeal for mootness, as might have been a normal procedure, but instead chose not to allow the lower court's opinion to stand unchallenged, and therefore vacated it before remanding the case to the district court. *(Hainsworth v. Martin)*.

In *Sims v. Baggett*, a federal district court in Alabama was considering a plan which combined three counties into one three-member representative district. Each county had a sufficient population to be an individual district. One of the counties had a Negro population of 71.9 per cent, while the others were predominantly white. The court held that the combination could not be explained on a "geometric, geographic or equalization basis" and therefore decided that the basis was clearly racial, and within the prohibition of *Gomillion v. Lightfoot*. It therefore refused to accept this part of the plan.

In *Holt v. Richardson*, the federal court in Hawaii stated that representative government required "apportionment which provides potentially equal representation to the divergent factors incorporated within the body politic . . ." This opinion appears to go beyond forbidding discrimination and toward requiring a proportional representation which borders on syndicalism.[1]

In conclusion it appears that the Supreme Court has not yet found a case in which it chooses to speak clearly on the subject of racial discrimination and apportionment. Until it does, a plan of apportionment which divides minority groups, or which overwhelms them in large multiple-member districts will be subject to attack. Furthermore, the attack will probably be successful if there is any indication of an intent to discriminate, or if there is not a sufficient explanation of the plan predicated on other factors.

Political Gerrymandering

/ *An apportionment plan should not be gerrymandered for partisan political advantage.*

There is still some legal doubt as to whether gerrymandering makes a plan unconstitutional, or whether that is a "political question" which the courts will refuse to consider. Obviously, however, in the interests of good government a plan should not be gerrymandered.

In *Reynolds v. Sims*, the Supreme Court condemned gerrymandering and approved the use of pre-existing political bound-

---

[1]Editorial note: Subsequently the Supreme Court has decided the Hawaiian case. It overruled the district court's objection to using registered voters rather than population data in casting districts. It did not give unqualified endorsement of the use of registered voters rather than population. It regarded Hawaii as unusual because of its large transient population and determined that in this instance the use of registered voters produced results not substantially different from one based on population. Manifestly the Court is aware that in some states use of registration data would produce results substantially different than the use of census data.

The Court also overruled the district court on the principle quoted above. To hold an apportionment invalid because it "potentially" may submerge minority groups is to rely on "conjecture rather than demonstrated facts" and to intrude on legislative prerogative. (*Burns v. Richardson*).

aries for legislative districts in the hope that such use would discourage gerrymandering.

A year later, in *Fortson v. Dorsey*, the Supreme Court commented that multiple-member districts might be used to "minimize or cancel out the voting strength of . . . political elements . . ." and said if that were proved, the Court would examine the record to determine if equal protection rights had been violated.

In *WMCA v. Lomenzo*, a federal court in New York held that an allegation of gerrymandering failed to raise a constitutional question. The Supreme Court affirmed that decision, *per curiam* without opinion. Justice Harlan said the court was affirming the holding that partisan gerrymandering did not violate the United States Constitution.

Other courts, however, such as the federal district court in Tennessee in *Baker v. Carr* have indicated that they will not approve a plan which uses multiple-member districts to discriminate against political elements.

As a result of these opinions, it has not been established whether partisan gerrymandering violates the Fourteenth amendment. But as a matter of political science, it is not conducive to good government, and federal courts will not be inclined to approve gerrymandered plans.

The charge has been made that the new Ohio apportionment is gerrymandered. However, boundaries were drawn along preexisting county, township, city and ward lines. And although it is true that single-member districts in Cuyahoga County may operate to some Republican advantage, such districts in Franklin and Hamilton Counties will operate to the advantage of the Democrats. In fact the Republicans in Franklin County felt so strongly about this that they filed an action in the Ohio Supreme Court trying to stop the plan. And there is another telling statistic which has not been used widely. In the more rural areas, where counties were combined, there are twenty districts which previously had forty-seven Republican legislators. Thus, had they all chosen to run again, forty-seven out-state Republican house members would have run against each other for twenty seats while at the same time only seven out-state incumbent Democrats would have been running against other Democrats.

Multiple-Member Districts

Multiple-member districts are not unconstitutional per se, but they make a plan subject to attack. Large multiple-member districts will probably not be allowed.

Another problem which is involved in creating an apportionment plan is whether to use multiple-member districts, or only single-member districts. In addition to the problems which multiple-member districts pose in regard to gerrymandering and racial discrimination, large multiple-member districts raise potential constitutional questions when they require long ballots or compose heavy voting units in the legislative body.

The Supreme Court commented upon this factor in *Lucas v. 44th General Assembly*. In Colorado, under both the then existing and the proposed apportionment plan, senators and representatives were elected at large from county-wide districts. Consequently, in Denver each elector voted for eight Senators and seventeen Representatives. The Supreme Court called this a "debatable feature" of the plan, noting that "an intelligent choice among candidates" was "made quite difficult."

However, in *Fortson v. Dorsey* the Supreme Court approved a Georgia plan for multiple-member districts. In doing so the court stated that it was merely holding that multiple-member districts were not unconstitutional *per se*, and that each such plan must be considered on its merits.

Of course, in *Reynolds v. Sims*, the court referred to the merits of drawing district boundaries along the lines of previously existing political subdivisions, so long as that policy does not result in deviations from substantially equal representation. This can result in multiple-member districts.

Courts have, however, questioned the legitimacy of apportionment plans which give one or a few large multi-member delegations a predominate voice in the legislature. For example, the federal court in Hawaii advised the legislature that it would never approve a plan under which 40 per cent of the Senate would come from one district and 36 per cent from another.[2]

As a result of these opinions, it appears that multiple-member districts are not invalid *per se*. However, they are convenient devices for smothering the voices of minority elements, whether racial or political, and when large enough they are conducive to a lack of effective representation and to the control of monolithic power groups which are capable of controlling legislative chambers. If any of these elements are present, it is evident that multiple-member districts are susceptible to constitutional attack.

An additional practical difficulty with multiple-member districts is that under some rules of computation they do not allow for as great a population deviation, within a given geographical district, as can be achieved by the use of single-member districts. An example is the 1963 decision of the federal district court in *Baker v. Carr*. In that case the court was calculating the degree of variation from the perfect district of multiple-member districts. For its computation, the court multiplied the number of people represented in the ideal district by the number of representatives, and then took the total average as the variation. Under this method the average was nearly 100 per cent, or one full ratio.

---

[2]Editorial note: The most significant Supreme Court pronouncement relative to multi-member districts is the Hawaiian case, handed down as this volume was being prepared. The Court reprimanded the district court for issuing the memorandum to the legislature expressing doubts concerning the validity of multi-member districts as an improper incursion on legislative prerogative, but it also ruled that the advice was erroneous. The Court emphasized that a state has a free choice regarding the use of multi-member districts; it may use them partially in a chamber, exclusively in a chamber, or even exclusively in both chambers. (All of the Hawaiian senate districts and most house districts are multi-member.)

"But the Equal Protection Clause does not require that at least one house of a bicameral legislature consist of single-member districts. Where the requirements of *Reynolds v. Sims* are met, apportionment schemes including multi-member districts will constitute invidious discrimination only if it can be shown that 'designedly or otherwise, a multi-member constituency apportionment scheme, under the circumstances of a particular case, would operate to minimize or cancel out the voting strength of racial or political elements of the voting population.' "

Nor is there any constitutional limit on the size of multi-member districts. "It may be that this invidious effect can more easily be shown if, in contrast to the facts in *Fortson,* districts are large in relation to the total number of legislators . . . . But the demonstration that a particular multi-member scheme effects an invidious result must appear from evidence on the record." (*Burns v. Richardson*).

Another method of making such a computation, which has been used by some courts, is to divide the total number of representatives within the district into the total population of the district, thus, in effect, computing how many people are represented by each legislator. This figure is then compared to the number represented in the perfect district, and the ratio of variance computed from it. Had such a method been used by the court in *Baker v. Carr*, mentioned above, the deviation would have been between 20 and 25 per cent rather than 100 per cent.

To illustrate this further, assume a perfect ratio of 100,000 and a maximum permissible variation of 15 per cent. A single-member district would be permissible if its population were between 85,000 and 115,000. Assuming the same variance ratio in a multiple-member district having five members, the population of that district, under the reasoning of *Baker v. Carr*, above, would have to be between 485,000 and 515,000. However, if that area were divided into single-member districts, each district could have a population of between 85,000 and 115,000, and the total population represented by the five districts could be anything between 425,000 and 575,000.

Thus, using the multiple-member district system, the amount of variation from the perfect district depends upon the method of computation used.

Terms for Sitting Legislators

Sitting legislators have no constitutional right to their office.

One of the most serious practical problems which arises with every reapportionment is that some sitting legislators must lose their seats. There can be no doubt that reapportionment denies to the state the services of many highly qualified and experienced legislators. Nevertheless, the courts have uniformly held that no legislator has a right to his seat and have not allowed such considerations to interfere with new apportionment plans.

Protection for sitting legislators takes two forms. The first is that new apportionment plans are drawn so that they interfere with as few sitting members as possible and avoid requiring sitting members to run against each other. When such considerations cause an apportionment plan to deviate beyond the 15 per cent population variance, or create a plan which lacks any other rational basis, the result is an unconstitutional plan which is of no benefit to anyone. *(League of Nebraska Municipalities v. Marsh).*

The second problem arises when a new apportionment cuts short the terms of incumbents. The courts have uniformly held in such cases that the terms of office end, and the legislators must run again in the new districts. For example, the federal court in Ohio cut short the term of Ohio Senators who were elected for four years, and ordered that those Senators who had two years of their terms remaining must nevertheless stand for election in 1966.

As the Oklahoma federal district court said *(Reynolds v. State Election Board),* ". . . no office holder has a vested right in an unconstitutional office any more than he has a right to be elected to that office. We believe that it would be invidiously discriminatory . . . we . . . declare all legislative offices of the Oklahoma legislature vacant . . ." Similar action was taken by the federal district court in Virginia, where it was affirmed by the Supreme Court *(Davis v. Mann),* and by the federal court in Hawaii.

Thus the interests of sitting legislators in preserving their seats cannot interfere with any of the other criteria which govern apportionment.

Conclusion

In summary, the following guidelines have been discussed:

1. Each legislator must represent approximately the same number of people. As a rule of thumb, a plan under which districts deviate from the population of the perfect district by no more than 15 per cent will be constitutional, and a plan having districts that exceed this 15 per cent limit will probably be unconstitutional.

2. An apportionment plan cannot be used for purposes of racial discrimination. Any plan which results in the power of minority groups being split between several districts, or overwhelmed in a multiple-member district by a monolithic majority, is likely to be held invalid.

3. As a strictly legal proposition, it is unclear whether political gerrymandering raises a judicial question, but the interests of good government obviously make gerrymandering an unacceptable practice.

4. Multiple-member districts are not unconstitutional *per se*. However, if used for purposes of racial discrimination, they will be unconstitutional. Additionally, if huge blocks of votes are seen in one district, it is not likely to meet court approval.

5. Sitting legislators have no constitutional right to their office. If an attempt to protect such legislators results in an apportionment plan that violates the other guidelines or which would continue in office legislators who were elected under an invalid system, then that plan is unconstitutional.

TABLE OF CASES

Baker v. Carr, 369 U.S. 691 (1962); 222 F. Supp. 684 (D.C. Tenn., 1963); 247 F. Supp. 629 (D.C. Tenn., 1965).

Burns v. Richardson, 384 U.S. 73, 16 L. Ed. 2d 376 (1966).

Buckley v. Hoff, 243 F. Supp. 873 (D.C. Vt., 1965).

Butcher v. Bloom, 203 A. 2d 556 (Pa., 1964).

Davis v. Mann, 377 U.S. 678 (1964); 379 U.S. 694 (1965).

Fortson v. Dorsey, 379 U.S. 433 (1965).

Gomillion v. Lightfoot, 364 U.S. 339 (1960).

Hainsworth v. Martin, 386 SW 2d 202 (Texas, 1965); 382 U.S. 109 (1965).

Holt v. Richardson, 240 F. Supp. 724 (D.C. Hawaii, 1965).

Honsey v. Donovan, 236 F. Supp. 8 (D.C. Minn., 1964).

Jackman v. Bodine, 208 A. 2d 648 (N.J., 1962).

League of Municipalities v. Marsh, 242 F. Supp. 357 (D.C. Neb., 1965).

Lucas v. 44th General Assembly of Colorado, 377 U.S. 713 (1964).

Nolan v. Rhodes, 378 U.S. 556 (1964); 251 F. Supp. 584 (D.C. Ohio, 1965); 86 S. Ct. 716 (1966).

Petuskey v. Rampton, 243 F. Supp. 365 (D.C. Utah, 1965).

Reynolds v. Sims, 377 U.S. 533 (1964).

Reynolds v. State Election Board, 233 F. Supp. 323 (D.C. Okla., 1964).

Shaefer v. Thomson, 240 F. Supp. 247 (D.C. Wyo., 1964); 251 F. Supp. 450 (D.C. Wyo., 1965).

Sims v. Baggett, 247 F. Supp. 96 (D.C. Ala., 1965).

Toombs v. Fortson, 241 F. Supp. 65 (D.C. Ga., 1963).

WMCA v. Lomenzo, 377 U.S. 633 (1964); 238 F. Supp. 916 (D.C. N.Y., 1965).

Wright v. Rockefeller, 376 U.S. 52 (1964).

chapter five

What Do Political Scientists Say?

Byron H. Marlowe

In the four year interval since *Baker v. Carr*, nearly forty states have revised their legislature and twenty-seven states, their congressional districts. This reapportionment wave presents an unusual opportunity for those political scientists interested in the subject of representation to share their knowledge and judgments about legislative apportionment. Unfortunately, the bulk of textbook references and journal articles on this subject have treated almost exclusively the "rural-urban" conflict over apportionment, usually documenting the disparities and occasionally devising measures of "malapportionment."[1] Some studies have enumerated and made generalizations about those criteria which were perceived as the *de facto* criteria employed in districting. One widely cited case study reported the dominant considerations as individual preservation, mutual preservation, political party preservation, and bloc

---

[1]Illustrative of this literature is Manning Dauer and Robert G. Kelsey, "Unrepresentative States," *National Municipal Review,* Dec., 1955, pp. 571-75. The most thorough discussion of statistical measures is Glendon Schubert and Charles Press, "Measuring Malapportionment," *American Political Science Review* June, 1964, pp. 302-27.

preservation.[2] Perusal of the literature shows that political scientists, as well as others, have said a lot about "malapportionment," but very little about what *ought* to be the criteria for apportioning legislatures.

To ascertain the criteria which those political scientists interested in representation and redistricting regard as valid and important, two mail survey samples were conducted.[3] A questionnaire of ninety-nine questions was mailed to those political scientists who have written books or articles on apportionment, appeared on panels, done unpublished research, or been directly involved in redistricting. A form of sixty-one questions was sent to a systematically selected random sample of people listed in the State and Local Government section of the 1961 Biographical Directory of the American Political Science Association. The return rate was 50 per cent for the long form and 80 per cent for the short form.

Appraisal of Reynolds v. Sims

All respondents were asked for their judgment of the one man-one vote doctrine of the Supreme Court in *Reynolds v. Sims*. Nearly 80 per cent of both samples regarded that ruling as "sound public policy." Less than 25 per cent in both samples favored a constitutional amendment that would allow "apportionment of one house of a bicameral legislature upon the basis of factors other than population."[4] The results of these two initial questions indicate the importance that political scientists attach to the population equality criterion.

A fundamental question posed by *Reynolds v. Sims* is how much latitude does its one man-one vote doctrine allow for the application of other criteria. Does it, operationally, prevent the use of other criteria? As Table 1 demonstrates, two-thirds of the respondents felt this ruling would allow application of other criteria.

---

[2] Gilbert Steiner and Samuel Gove, *The Legislature Redistricts Illinois* (Urbana: University of Illinois Press, 1956).
[3] The survey was conducted by Charles Barrell, Howard Hamilton, and the writer in January, 1966.
[4] The language of SJ Res. 2, the 1965 "Dirksen amendment."

TABLE 1

Application of Other Criteria Within "Population Equality"

	Per cent Yes	Random-Select
(1) Virtually precludes application of any other criteria.	31	26
(2) Allows some room for use of additional criteria.	37	28
(3) Allows some, but not enough room for additional criteria.	9	13
(4) Allows adequate scope for the application of other legitimate criteria.	20	28
(5) No answer.	3	6

If the "population equality" rule in operation precludes application of other considerations, then our question of what *ought* to be the criteria would be irrelevant. About 30 per cent of the respondents gave that judgment, but the majority indicated that there remains some room for other criteria. About 10 per cent thought insufficient room, but one-fifth to one-fourth thought that there is adequate scope for application of other "legitimate criteria." Some respondents who checked the first option may have been influenced by an intense adherence to the population criterion, perhaps regarding it as the only legitimate consideration. It is the writer's observation that the requirement of population equality will never cause a legislature to eschew other considerations when drawing district lines. In this regard it may be noted that the opinion of the Supreme Court in *Reynolds v. Sims* acknowledged the legitimacy of other criteria and mentioned some which might justify minor deviation from absolute population equality.

Atypical Districting Systems

There are ways of achieving mathematically equal representation of population without establishing districts of equal population.

Judgment was asked for on four unusual districting systems that attempt to accomplish equality of representation without using equally populated districts. These systems differ from the "little federal plan" which bases one house on population and the other on geographical areas. The theoretical advantage of these plans is that they would allow counties or definable communities to be used as legislative districts. Two such arrangements have prevailed in one or more states for generations; the other two have been recently enacted by some legislatures, but have been declared unconstitutional by disapproving courts. The select sample, the recipients of the long questionnaire, were asked to evaluate these four atypical patterns.

1. Bicameral Offset. This is the frequently discussed idea of compensating for the under-representation of a district in one chamber by over-representation in the other, an idea mentioned by the Supreme Court in *Reynolds v. Sims*. It achieves population equality by averaging the two chambers together. One can easily surmise why this arrangement was overwhelmingly disapproved. A bicameral system permits each chamber to exercise a veto over the other; therefore, a community might find its interests thwarted by the under-representation in one chamber. Additionally, the offset to be exact would require congruent house and senate districts which rarely occur.

2. Weighted and Fractional Voting. In a weighted voting system a representative would be given the number of votes in the legislature to which his representative unit would be entitled in order to equally represent population. A fractional voting system would assign representatives fractions of a vote for fractions of population in districts that could otherwise be represented only by combining districts or changing boundaries. The fractional system was slightly more acceptable than the weighted system. The most obvious weakness of these plans is that they greatly exaggerate the importance of voting within the legislature. The voting power of the representative would be equalized, yet this is only one of the series of steps in the legislative process and often the least important step. Obvious difficulties appear in attempts to equalize power on committees, to ensure adequate access for constituents in the larger districts, and to prevent interest groups from concentrating on a few key legislators. Thus, the judgment of the political science profession is that "one man—one

vote" should apply within the legislature as well as for the constituents.

3. Overlapping Districts. A so-called "floterial" district has been used to combine a smaller county with a larger neighboring one, which already had one or more representatives, to form a new district. For example, if one legislator is to represent 30,000 people and county A has a population of 50,000 and county B 10,000, county A would have one representative and a combined district of A and B one representative. The disadvantage of this plan is the distinct possibility that operationally the larger county will end up with two representatives and the smaller county with none. This seems particularly undesirable where there are differing values in each county, e.g., a rural-urban division.

4. Equalization Over a Decade—the Ohio "floating fraction." Until 1966 Ohio maintained or combined counties as districts and represented fractions of the population over the average size district. Ohio authorized an additional representative for a given term (two years) for each additional one-fifth district population. Thus, a district with one-fifth more population than the average per representative would have two representatives during one term, and one representative for the other four terms of that decade. In this system each fractional district is both over-represented and under-represented during the decade.

None of these atypical systems received as high as a 25 per cent endorsement. Thus, it was the judgment of the respondents that population equality should prevail in each session, in each chamber, and in each district.

What Is "Substantial Equality"?

The Supreme Court has declined to define "substantial equality" in mathematical terms. If other districting criteria are disregarded, districts can be drawn with less than one per cent divergence between populations; however, if city or county boundaries are used faithfully, a few districts with conspicuous population deviations may be inexorable. In public discussion of the proper standard for "substantial equality," a 15 per cent maximum population deviation is frequently mentioned, and in recent litigation, the lower federal courts have occasionally adverted to it. However, the 15 per cent figure originated in 1950 from a committee of the

American Political Science Association as a proposed standard for congressional districts and its appropriateness for state legislative districts is at least controvertible.[5]

Anyone who has experimented with districting is aware that the 15 per cent maximum is more easily achieved in drawing congressional districts than state districts, and it complicates the drawing of state districts if local jurisdictional lines are used. Of course, a 15 per cent deviation does allow a 30 per cent maximum difference between the largest and smallest districts. Whether from inertia, suggestion, or reflection, this 15 per cent standard was endorsed by a majority of the respondents, although 40 per cent of the random sample felt that it was too great to achieve population equality. Thus, the judgment must be that 15 per cent is the acceptable maximum limit, but this limit should be reached only in unusual cases which cannot achieve greater population equality without great difficulty.

TABLE 2

Maximum Allowable Population Deviation per District

	Per cent of Samples	
	Random	Select
Deviation up to 10%	39	30
Deviation up to 15%	38	48
Deviation up to 20%	9	9
Deviation up to 25%	1	2
Deviation up to 50%	1	0
No answer	12	11

Apportioning Criteria—Rank

Respondents were asked to evaluate a list of twenty-three specific criteria as valid or invalid (i.e., proper or improper) and to classify those deemed valid as "Very Important," "Desirable," or "Permissible." In order to tabulate the order of the preferences,

---

[5]Committee on Reapportionment of Congress, "The Reapportionment of Congress," *American Political Science Review,* March, 1951, p. 155.

a value of three points was assigned to each "Very important," two points for each "Desirable," and one point for each "Permissible." The results are presented in Table 3.

The few criteria which most respondents deemed valid and very important are the means and ends of fair and objective districting. The only criteria commanding virtual unanimity are the traditional standards frequently mandated by Congress for casting congressional districts—compact and symmetrical districts of equal population. Perhaps many respondents assumed that these criteria would automatically accomplish the third ranking criterion, averting minority party control of the legislature.

Consistent with the judgment of most respondents that "substantial equality" of population does not prevent the use of other criteria, most of the respondents approved the use of political subdivisions and consideration of economic, social, and regional interests. Those criteria, however, were marked as valid by two-thirds of the sample, but received only about 40 per cent of the possible points.

There was also broad agreement that the criteria at the bottom of Table 3 are invalid. These items are the antithesis of equitable and objective districting; however, there is considerable evidence that they are important to legislators and frequently are paramount considerations in districting. There is a contrast in the norms of politicians and professors, or perhaps between the norms of politicians and the public.

When non-population factors are acceptable they are those most compatible with a 15 per cent population deviation per district. Criteria such as maintaining political subdivisions as representative units, and considerations of economic, social and regional interests ranked fourth and fifth as acceptable criteria. Not dividing counties, and following county, city, township, ward lines even at some reduction of population equality, two factors less compatible with population equality, ranked much lower, tenth and fourteenth.

Table 3 reflects an absence of consensus on several items. Only five criteria were supported as valid by a majority of the random sample. However, the results for some of the items in the low agreement range may be misleading. "Fostering competitive districts" and "fostering a strong block of minority members" scored 43 per cent and 30 per cent valid; yet, few if any respondents are opposed to competitive districts or a strong opposition party. How-

TABLE 3

Rank Order of Apportioning Criteria By Total Points—Random Sample

Rank Order	Criteria	Random Sample	
		Per cent Valid	Total Points
1	Population equality	99	256
2	Compactness and symmetry	95	200
3	Averting minority party control of legislature	70	164
4	Maintaining political subdivisions as representative units	65	116
5	Consideration of economic, social, and regional interests	63	112
6	Partisan neutrality	45	95
7[a]	Fostering a statewide distribution of seats by party generally proportional to vote	49	86
8[a]	Fostering competitive districts	43	86
9	Elimination of multi-member districts	43	85
10	Not dividing counties	46	77
11	Assuring some seats for the minority party within each metropolitan county	35	72
12	Maximizing heterogeneous districts	35	68
13[a]	Utilization of multi-member districts	46	66
14[a]	Following county, city, twp., ward lines even at some reduction of population equality	41	66
15	Fostering a strong block of minority members	30	56
16	Maximizing homogeneous districts	26	46
17	Minimizing the number of constituents per legislator	26	43
18[b]	Assuring ethnic minorities control of some districts	25	26
19[b]	Interest of incumbents	25	26
20	Advantage of majority party	12	20
21	At least one seat for every county	10	16
22	Fostering the strength of residents outside the metropolises	11	13
23	Fostering safe districts	9	8

(N = 92, 276 total possible points)

[a] Total point tie broken by highest percentage marking as valid.
[b] Total point and per cent valid ties broken by lowest per cent marking as invalid.

ever, half or more reject these as conscious goals in the design of districts. We also find that heterogeneous districts are only slightly favored over homogeneous ones, and elimination of multi-member districts only marginally differs from their utilization. Only the choice between safe and competitive districts shows any significant agreement. Any redistricting plan will inevitably accomplish some of the other criteria listed in Table 3; however, it is the judgment of our samples that these should be by-products of seeking an objective application of population equality, compactness, and symmetry.

Districts: SMD v. MMD

Forty-three per cent of the random sample in Table 3 checked "elimination of multi-member districts" as a valid criterion whereas 46 per cent checked "utilization of multi-member districts," but the point totals for both are low. This could be read as indifference, or indecision about the relative merits of multi-member and single-member districts. However, we found that few respondents wanted to make an either-or choice.

TABLE 4

Preference of Single-Member or Multi-Member Districts

	Select Sample
Universal SMD	26%
General use of SMD	48%
General use of MMD	6%
Universal MMD	2%
No answer	18%

The select sample was asked to pass judgment on this question by selecting one of the four choices in Table 4 to the question: "Legislative districts should be............" The results reveal a much stronger preference for single-member districts than was indicated in Table 3, although only a minority of the respondents favored universal use of either system. These results correspond to the prevailing practice in the country. A few states have only multi-member districts; single-member district is the predominant pattern, but most states have both.

Homogeneous or Heterogeneous Districts

It is frequently asserted that homogeneous districts facilitate representation, because community sentiments are more clearly defined. Thus, it is argued that the districting pattern should segregate rural, urban, and suburban areas. However, one also hears impressive arguments that heterogeneous constituencies are more conducive to the legislative process. Responses in Table 3 to this choice are rather inconclusive: 35 per cent indicating a preference for heterogeneous districts and 26 per cent for homogeneous.

TABLE 5

Heterogeneous versus Homogeneous Districts

	Pct. of Select Sample		
	Yes	No	NA
Generally, representative government can best be realized by drawing *homogeneous* districts.	33	43	24
Heterogeneous districts are more desirable constituencies.	37	37	26
In metropolitan areas there should be separate districts for the core, the outer wards, and the suburbs.	30	43	28
In a metropolitan area districts might appropriately be radian segments, even at some sacrifice of compactness or symmetry.	43	41	17
Districts should be drawn without reference to homogeneity or heterogeneity.	30	43	28

The select sample was asked the questions in Table 5; the results disclose sharp disagreement. Only a third of the respondents would disregard this consideration when apportioning; however, the respondents disagree about which goal to choose. Overall the returns show slightly more preference for heterogeneous districts. Most respondents disapproved of segregating the core, outer wards, and suburbs of metropolitan areas. Many respondents, however, endorsed the novel suggestion of radian style districts to achieve heterogeneity.

Minorities

A specific category of this issue is whether and how to relate districting to ethnic and socio-economic minorities, an issue which is likely to generate heat in the districting of any metropolis. A familiar demand of minorities is that they should be predominant in some districts, where they can elect their "own," rather than being submerged in a large district or fragmented and submerged in several districts. This poses questions which entail judgments about the nature of the political process. What arrangements maximize the political leverage of minorities? Is one's "own" rep-

TABLE 6

What Consideration of Minorities?

	Per cent of Samples			
	Random		Select	
	Yes	No	Yes	No
Minorities, particularly ethnic, should be assured representation by designing districts in which they will be preponderant.	16	79	30	56
Minorities are better served by not being concentrated in a district.	58	27	37	35
Minorities are better served by not being concentrated in a district *only* if districts are competitive.	42	33	31	30
The location of minorities should be disregarded; "reverse discrimination" is illegitimate.	67	23	43	35

resentative essential for effective representation? Is the cost of securing one's "own" representative likely to be a diminution of the minority's political leverage? It also poses a serious question of social ethics: should districting be "color blind" and oblivious of class?

To elicit judgments on this topic, respondents were asked the four items of Table 6. This was the only segment of the questionnaire which produced sharp differences between the samples. The random sample strongly disapproved of designing districts to achieve a minority group's preponderance, thought that this should not be a consideration, and felt that such segregation would not be to a minority's best interest. The select sample was much more in favor of relating districts to such factors.

Districting Agency

There was substantial agreement that districting should employ "automatic and impersonal procedures which minimize discretion" (61 per cent yes), rather than being done by the legislature vested with "broad discretion" (22 per cent yes). However, only 41 per cent favored use of a computer "programmed to maximize compactness and population equality"; the others evidently favor consideration of personal judgments, and additional criteria, or perhaps are skeptical of gadgetry.

The usual method to make districting automatic and impersonal is to include a districting formula in the state constitution. However, even a constitutional districting formula is likely to allow, or even require, judgments when drawing specific district lines. Traditionally, districting is a legislative function, but only one-fourth of our samples favored this practice even with a constitutional formula. Both samples, as shown in Table 7, ranked the legislature second behind nonpartisan citizen boards when asked who should implement the constitutional formula.

Many respondents stated that the legislature is overly concerned with protecting its members. That factor and the possibility that the legislature may default perhaps are the reasons that some states have assigned the districting function to an administrative official, usually governor or secretary of state, or an ex-officio board as in Ohio. Recently two states, Illinois and Michigan, have vested the function in a bi-partisan apportionment commission nominated by the state party organizations. Neither of these alternatives received much support from respondents. An elective officer or

TABLE 7

Choice of Apportioning Agency to Implement Constitutional Formula

Agent	Per cent of Samples Random	Select
Nonpartisan citizen board	45	30
Legislature	25	24
Bi-partisan board	9	9
Elective officer or board	4	17
Other and no answer	17	20

ex-officio board may not be free of partisanship. The members of a bi-partisan apportionment board will be intense partisans and the result may be deadlock, as has occurred in Michigan and Illinois.

A few respondents suggested courts or civil servants as apportioning agents. Neither of these appear very feasible. In some or most states, the civil service probably lacks sufficient public confidence to be vested with this function. Courts are loathe to undertake any nonjudicial function and are not eager to engage in apportionment. Their proper role is to exercise judicial review to assure that population equality and other requirements of a state's constitution are fulfilled.

The nonpartisan citizens board, the agency with the most endorsement in this survey, is rather novel. During the current reapportionment wave, citizen boards have been used in an advisory capacity by some legislatures and courts, but Alaska is the only state which vests authority in such a board. The Alaskan apportionment board prepares a redistricting plan and submits it to the governor for promulgation. He may modify the board's plan if he states his reasons in the promulgation message. The

Alaskan arrangement is recommended by the National Municipal
League in the latest edition of its *Model State Constitution.*[6]

---

[6]Sixth edition (1963), pp. 45-49.

chapter six

The Criteria of the Ohio Constitutional Convention of 1850-1851

Stewart R. Jaffy

In order to understand the basis for Article XI of the Ohio Constitution, which sets out the apportionment of the Ohio House of Representatives and the Ohio Senate, some historical background is in order.

Even before Ohio became a state its inhabitants were entitled to representation in the territorial legislature on a population only basis.[1] Upon admission of Ohio into the Union, representation in both houses continued to be based solely on population.[2] This constitutional guaranty of numerical equality in representation was in fact honored, but nevertheless apportionment of the Ohio Legislature was completely unsatisfactory in the first half of the nineteenth century since no standards other than equality were prescribed, and the apportionment power in the hands of the state legislature became a politician's dream and a voter's nightmare.

---

[1] Article II of the Articles of Compact of the Ordinance of the Northwest Territory of 1787.
[2] Ohio Constitution of 1802, Sections 2 and 6.

For example, the Ohio Supreme Court, in 1853, commenting on the failure of the apportionment system under the constitution of 1802 said:[3]

"The State has been subjected to a most humiliating experience, while the power was left with the General Assembly and the scenes of anarchy and confusion, which had marked its exercise there, undoubtedly determined the people to deprive that body of it absolutely, so far as the election of their own members was concerned for the future."

The foregoing quotation is probably the best explanation of the overriding feeling of the members of the constitutional convention as to an apportionment plan. They were not happy with the way apportionment had been conducted in the past. They wanted a system which would be automatic or self-executing, which would eliminate the political bickering which is normal where the discretion in drawing lines is left to a legislature. They wanted to avoid gerrymandering.

Thus, the plan designed by the constitutional convention was based on specific requirements which a board was given to follow without discretion.

Ohio Supreme Court Judge Ranney, a delegate to the Convention of 1851, in a case following the convention described the new apportionment provisions as follows:[4]

"And, first, the Constitution apportions political power amongst the *inhabitants* of the state, as nearly equally as possible, in proportion to numbers, without any regard whatever to property, or, indeed to any other circumstance. Inhabitants alone are represented: a given number in one place exercise the same political power, as a like number in any other locality. I am aware that some departure from the absolute equality on numbers is allowed in favor of the inhabitants of small counties, in the constitution for the House of Representatives; but this in no *wise* changes the *basis* of representation from population to property."

The "departure from the absolute equality of numbers" mentioned by Judge Ranney was the provision in the Constitution which entitled counties with a one-half ratio of population to have one representative.

---

[3]*State ex rel. Dudley v. Evans,* 1 O.S. 422,443 (1853).
[4]*Dudley v. Evans, Supra.*

It was their search for apportionment based on equality of population that caused the delegates to the Convention of 1851 to devise the fractional representation system. The Convention was in general agreement that the criteria for representation should be population. On the other hand, it was quite divided in how this goal should be achieved. One faction in the Convention proposed single-member districts as an answer to equal representation. Another faction successfully opposed this proposal on the grounds that no impartial agency could be found to subdivide counties into single-member districts.

The spectre of gerrymandering overshadowed the whole Convention. Past experience with politically inspired apportionment plans promulgated by the General Assembly had caused a furor in the State. Delegate Reemelin, an advocate of the single-member district plan vividly described past legislative maneuverings.[5]

> "Apportionments have been arranged by a very few men, perhaps very often by a single chairman of a committee, sitting in his room at a hotel, taking a map in his hand, not asking himself, what will be for the good of the people? . . . what apportionment will give the best chance for a fair representation? He asks himself no such question, but goes to marking upon the map his black lines, and red lines and blue lines, to see how by an apportionment some particular party, or some favorite object can be best subserved and sustained. And when the report would come in here all kinds of party feeling would be excited; and it would be obvious to everyone, that, not the interests of the people, but the interest of men . . . of private and particular individuals and parties only were at stake."
> I believe that the history of nearly every apportionment in the state, will bear me out in the statements of fact, that unfair apportionments more than everything else, have been the fruitful cause of the political ill-feeling, excitement and enmity, which should never be encouraged in the State of Ohio."

The stumbling block to the single-member district apportionment plans was the creation of an impartial tribunal to subdivide the counties. The Convention discussed use of township trustees, county commissioners, and even a local board composed of representatives of the people in different townships and wards as agencies to create single-member districts. All of these schemes were rejected. Mr. Dorsey, a member of the Committee on Appor-

---

[5]*Constitution Convention Proceeding,* 1851, Volume 1, p. 100.

tionment, probably summed it up best as to why a fractional plan was adopted when he said:[6]

> "It is proper for me to state a large number of the committee on apportionment, were strongly in favor of the single member district system, and the subject was commended to the favorable vote of the committee by the opinions of the members of the convention. But I have been induced to believe, that while the plan that we have reported approximates in a very considerable degree such system, it obviates the objections that would arise, were the principle of single districts fully carried out.
>
> Gentlemen may say what they please about the facility with which counties and cities may be divided, but I say, that when they attempt it, they will find that it is a difficult matter. In order that it may be done, there must be power somewhere, and whatever that power may be, it will be subject to political influences; and our intention has been, so far as possible to get rid of such influences."

Judge Ranney, then Delegate Ranney, speaking to the Convention against single-member district plan said:

> "Now I never heard that there was any demand for this cutting up of territory; and if there is one sentiment in the State that is universal in one party and nearly so in the other, it is against this cutting up of counties. It was once tried in the General Assembly, and the result was a commotion and nearly a revolution; and so great was the political indignation upon the subject, that the legislature was forced to retrace its steps."

A review of the Convention Proceedings shows that Ohio's apportionment plan as contained in our present Constitution was based on two principles—equality of population and maintenance of the integrity of the counties to keep gerrymandering at an absolute minimum.

Thus, it may be said that the members of the constitutional convention made the following basic policy decisions as to apportionment of the Ohio legislature:

1. The apportionment formula should be spelled out in the constitution.
2. The application of the formula should be a ministerial function only, leaving virtually no discretion to those who were to apply the formula.

---

[6]*Constitutional Convention Proceedings,* 1851, Volume 2, p. 758.

3. Reapportionment should occur every ten years following the federal census.
4. Counties should be preserved as units of representation with provision for creating legislative districts out of two or more whole counties in the more sparsely populated areas of the State.
5. Under no conditions were county lines to be crossed in creating districts.
6. The basis of representation in both houses was to be population only.
7. The relatively insignificant disparities in representation that necessarily resulted from the maintenance of county lines were to be balanced out by providing for additional representatives or senators in one or more sessions during the decennium for the population in excess of the so-called ratio of representation.

Subsequent Developments; Amendment and Litigation

The apportionment system designed in 1851 operated satisfactorily and did not engender many disputes. The Apportionment Board performed its ministerial duties each decade, and thus Ohio has been one of the few states which has reapportioned regularly without a single default. Litigation of Article XI was minimal; only three suits were instituted before 1961.[7]

As to rates of representation, Article XI *has been amended only once*, the so-called Hanna amendment in 1903, which provided that every county should be a House district with at least one representative.[8] Previously a county's population had to be one-half of the ratio of representation to be entitled to a seat. Initially, the effect of the Hanna amendment was insubstantial, only ten of the eighty-eight counties had populations less than one-half ration, but by 1961 there were forty-eight such counties and tremendous disparities in representation. Whereas in 1961 Vinton County had a population of 10,274 and one representative, Lake

---

[7]*State ex rel. v. Campbell,* 48 O.S. 435 (1891); *State ex rel. Herbert v. Bricker,* 139 O.S. 499 (1942); *State ex rel. Lehman v. DiSalle,* 173 O.S. 361 (1962).
[8]The Article XI policy of not dividing counties was challenged sporadically; proposals to establish single-member districts universally were rejected three times by the electorate and also by the constitutional convention of 1874.

County had a population of 148,700 and only one representative. By 1961 a majority of the House members were elected by districts aggregating only 28.4 per cent of the population of the state. Thus, over six decades the Hanna amendment progressively nullified the paramount original objective of Article XI: equality of representation.

The gross disparities eventually led to the Nolan lawsuit in 1961 challenging the constitutionality of the Hanna amendment as a denial of "equal protection." The federal court reasoned that "equal protection" was satisfied if one chamber of a legislature were apportioned according to population (a view taken by several courts prior to *Reynolds v. Sims*). Because the Senate was apportioned strictly by population, the court ruled that the inequalities in the House were permissible.[9] Its decision, however, was overruled by the Supreme Court on the basis of its holding in *Reynolds* that both chambers must adhere to the population principle.[10]

Thereupon the district court directed the legislature to reapportion the House without reference to the Hanna provision. Such a plan was adopted by the Ohio General Assembly at a special session. The plan provided, among other things, for the splitting of counties for representation purposes. The plan was voted on in May, 1965, and was rejected. Thereafter, various proposals for apportionment were considered by committees of the Ohio General Assembly, but the legislature was unable to agree upon a new plan.

In the meantime, in July 1965, another suit was filed challenging the apportionment of the Ohio Senate. One of the complaints in that suit was aimed at the floating fraction system, the equalization method devised by the 1851 convention.

The federal court agreed with the plaintiff.[11]

. . . the provision (Ohio Cons., Art. XI, Sec. 6a) providing for a varying number of Senators from the same district for different sessions during a decennial period results in under-representation for some sessions and over-representation for others, but never for reasonably exact representation; that the provisions of the Ohio Constitution that require said malapportionment of the Senate as above related, are in violation of the Fourteenth Amendment to

[9]*Nolan v. Rhodes,* 218 F. Supp. 953 (1963), Rev'd. 378 U.S. 556 (1964).
[10]378 U.S. 556 (1964).
[11]*Blosser v. Rhodes,* 251 F. Supp. 584 (1965). This was a reversal of its explicit holding in *Nolan v. Rhodes* in 1963.

the Constitution of the United States and are therefore null and void.

The federal court proceeded to invite all parties to the lawsuits and all other interested parties to submit a plan for apportioning the legislature. Over twenty plans were submitted to the Court.

The court then issued an order of apportionment for the 1966 election, adopting the plan prepared by the State Apportionment Board. This plan cuts across county lines and establishes single-member districts.

The Blosser case had been consolidated with the Nolan case. Subsequent to the apportionment order, the case was appealed to the United States Supreme Court. The plaintiff, Nolan, in his brief on appeal contended that the court had erred in its judgment of the Senate and the floating fraction, that Article XI without the Hanna provision was constitutional, and that the court should have promulgated an apportionment only for the House and that in conformity with Article XI except for the Hanna provision.[12] The Supreme Court, however, affirmed the judgment of the lower court.

Thus, for the moment Ohio has an apportionment plan. Some observers believe the next General Assembly will submit a plan for apportionment to the people; others feel that the federal court will need to make further apportionment orders.

---

[12]Appellant brief, *Nolan v. Rhodes,* 86 S. Ct. 716 (1966).

chapter seven

The Election System and the Party System

Thomas A. Flinn

Election systems today are asked to meet the criterion "one man-one vote."[1] The demand is for political equality, and it is hard to resist; however, election systems may be asked to serve other principles which are also hard to deny. One is the principle of majority rule which requires that the alternatives preferred by the largest number of people be chosen. These alternatives may be conceived of as alternative policies or as alternative governments. The definition which causes least difficulty is that majority rule is a principle which requires that the alternative government, which is preferred by the largest number of people, be chosen. Another principle an election system may be asked to serve is that of minority rights, a complicated notion which in this case means simply minority representation. The minority need not be represented exactly according to its numerical strength, but well enough to make its case known.

It seems to require no special argument to maintain that an election system should serve the principles of political equality, majority rule, and minority representation. In fact, it seems obvious; yet the most zealous advocates of reapportionment have

---

[1] The term "electoral system" is used in this chapter, because the writer is examining the electoral effects of representation systems.

been much concerned with political equality and not much concerned with any other principle. The likely explanation is that they have assumed that an election system that provided political equality would also provide majority rule, at least. Under one condition, anyway, that assumption is correct barring districting of grotesque proportions, and that condition is political division along urban-rural lines.

Another assumption seemingly made by many who have stressed only political equality is that state politics do reveal persistent urban-rural cleavages. But is that true? The making of an answer requires study of what goes on in state politics, particularly in state legislatures. A few years ago the writer undertook a study of the Ohio General Assembly and reported some of the results in a form somewhat different from what follows here.[2] The study was prompted by contradictory observations concerning divisions in the Ohio legislature. Some journalists covering the scene spoke of the "cornstalk brigade," meaning a tight rural faction which was thought to be dominant. On the other hand, party caucuses were mentioned, and party voting certainly occurred sometimes.

The method of the investigation was roll call analysis. It was realized, of course, that roll call votes are but one aspect of legislative life, but it is an important one. And it is reasonable to believe that important divisions will be revealed by voting decisions on roll calls. Four sessions of the General Assembly were selected for consideration: 1935, 1949, 1955, and 1957. Only the findings for 1949 and 1957 will be referred to, but let it be said that the findings for the other two sessions are generally consistent with them. In 1949 the governor and legislature were Democratic, and in 1957 they were Republican.

Every roll call in the selected sessions was inspected, but unanimous or nearly unanimous votes were rejected since they would not, of course, reveal divisions of any kind. To put it differently, only controversial roll calls were retained for study, and they were defined as the roll calls on which the minority was equal to 10 per cent or more of the majority. In 1949 there were 216 controversial roll calls in the House and 149 in the Senate. In the 1957 session the numbers were 173 and 83 respectively. It may be added

---

[2]The earlier report is "The Outline of Ohio Politics," *Western Political Quarterly* (September, 1960), pp. 702-721.

by way of explanation that the number of controversial roll calls is generally much larger when the Democrats are in control.

The legislature was then divided into four groups: urban Democrats, urban Republicans, rural Democrats, and rural Republicans. Urban members were those from counties classified by the Census Bureau as standard metropolitan areas or as parts of standard metropolitan areas. All other members were said to be rural. The reason for classifying legislators in this way was to make it possible to separate the effect of area from the effect of party. It was suspected, for example, that some unwary observers had described situations in which rural members mostly Republican had opposed urban members mostly Democratic as urban-rural factionalism whereas it was equally possible that the conflict was partisan. The number of legislators in each group is shown in the table below.

TABLE 1

Composition of the Ohio General Assembly, 1949 and 1957 Sessions

	Group							
Year	House					Senate		
	UD	UR	RuD	RuR		UD	UR	RuD	RuR
1949	51	12	18	54		18	3	1	11
1957	31	38	11	59		12	10	0	12

Legend: D=Democrats; R=Republicans; U=Urban; Ru=Rural.

The voting position of each group was compared with that of every other group in the same body whenever possible. Rural Democrats in the Senate were so few in the 1949 and 1957 sessions that it was not possible to compare them with any other group. The measure was a very simple statistical device called the index of likeness. It is a single numerical expression indicating the degree to which the position of two voting groups is the same or different. It is calculated by subtracting the per cent of yea votes cast by one group from the per cent of yea votes cast by another group (always subtracting the smaller number from the larger) and by subtracting the result from 100. Thus, if the first group is unanimously in favor of a proposal and a second is unanimously against, the index of likeness is 0. If both are 75 per cent in favor, the index of likeness is 100. If one is 80 per cent in favor and the other is 80 per cent opposed, the index is 40 which may seem to be fairly high but is really indicative of a sharp division between the groups. An index as high as 60 also indicates division although not so sharp since it could be produced by one group voting more than 2 to 1 in one direction and by another group voting more than 2 to 1 in the other directions.

Findings are reported in the next table.

TABLE 2

Distribution of Indices of Likeness Expressing the Relation of Groups in the Ohio General Assembly, 1949 and 1957 Sessions

Groups	Per Cent of Roll Calls in Given Ranges						
	0-19	20-39	40-59	60-79	80-100	(M)	(N)
1949 House							
UD/UR	12	14	13	18	42	63	216
RuD/RuR	15	12	15	26	32	59	216
UD/RuD	0	3	5	18	73	89	216
UR/RuR	0	2	6	21	71	84	216
1949 Senate							
UD/UR	24	22	14	16	25	46	149
UR/RuR	3	5	9	22	61	80	149
1957 House							
UD/UR	8	4	10	26	53	73	173
RuD/RuR	9	9	13	29	40	67	173
UD/RuD	1	8	14	22	56	75	173
UR/RuR	0	1	5	18	76	85	173
1957 Senate							
UD/UR	17	14	21	24	23	54	83
UR/RuR	0	2	6	30	61	83	83

Legend: D=Democrats; R=Republicans; U=Urban; Ru=Rural.
M=Mean Index; N=Number of Controversial Roll Calls in Session.

Note: Failure of per cent figures in any row to total 100 is due to rounding.

The urban-rural factionalism thesis would have it that urban legislators are united despite party differences as are rural legislators. This thesis predicts also that Democrats and Republicans will both be disunited with the line of division being the line between city and country. However, the facts as shown in Table 2 are contrary to what is predicted by the urban-rural factionalism thesis.

First, sharp conflict as indicated by the frequence of roll calls with indices of likeness below 40 is fairly common when urban Democrats are compared with urban Republicans and when rural Democrats are compared with rural Republicans. Six such comparisons are provided in the table. There is variation, but the median per cent of roll calls with indices below 40 is 28 per cent.

Second, clear differences as indicated by the frequence of roll calls with indices of likeness below 60 are certainly common when urban Democrats are compared with Republicans from urban areas and when rural Democrats are compared with Republicans from rural areas. For the six relevant comparisons in Table 2, from 22 per cent to 60 per cent of the roll calls show indices of likeness of less than 60. The median is 40.5 per cent.

Third, sharp conflict as indicated by the frequence of roll calls with indices of likeness below 40 is rare when urban Democrats are compared with rural Democrats and when urban Republicans are compared with rural Republicans. Nine per cent is the highest frequence, and the median is 2.5 per cent.

Fourth, clear differences between the urban and rural wings of each party as indicated by the frequence of roll calls with indices of likeness of less than 60 are not common. Such roll calls typically constitute less than 10 per cent of the controversial roll calls in any session with the median being 8 per cent. Consideration of the six relevant comparisons shows there are at least two exceptions. One is the relation between urban Republicans and rural Republicans in the Senate during the 1949 session: 17 per cent of the roll calls had indices under 60, which is almost double the mean for the four sessions which were analyzed. The other exception is the relation between urban Democrats and rural Democrats in the 1957 House: 23 per cent of the roll calls had indices under 60; but this is about 50 per cent over the mean for four sessions.

What may be said in summary is that the relations necessary to support the urban-rural factionalism thesis do not exist. Instead the data show that Democrats and Republicans are frequently in conflict even if they come from the same areas and that each party is internally united despite the existence of urban and rural wings.

These relations between legislative groups are not peculiar to Ohio. An extended study of legislative politics in Illinois and Missouri led to the conclusion that there was no support for the notion that those legislatures were characterized by urban-rural conflict and dominated by rural members.[3] An analysis of the Indiana legislature disclosed that party membership is the major correlate of roll calls, not metropolitan or non-metropolitan residence.[4] A study of voting in the Alabama legislature turned up little evidence showing significant urban-rural divisions, but showed instead that the legislature tended to divide into pro-administration and anti-administration groups.[5] Malcolm Jewell has found that on the basis of evidence from a number of states party conflict is fairly common, although the level varies.[6]

The next question is whether election systems that provide political equality also provide majority rule and minority representation when the alternative governments are not urban and rural factions, but instead are rival political parties. The answer is that they might, but that under some conditions they will not. These conditions which cancel any equivalence between political equality on the one hand and majority rule and minority representation on the other will be called "frustrating conditions."

One such frustrating condition occurs when the more popular party wins some seats with majorities much larger than needed ("surplus majorities") and loses the majority of seats, but in the aggregate by a fairly small margin. The number of voters behind each elected representative may be even precisely equal, but majority rule is blocked. Another frustrating condition occurs when the voters supporting each of the contending parties are equally distributed among the electing districts. The party (assuming there are only two) receiving in excess of 50 per cent of all the votes will also win every district. There will be a huge "majority bonus" and no representation of the minority. Of course, it is unlikely that

[3]David R. Derge, "Metropolitan and Outstate Alignments in Illinois and Missouri Legislative Delegations," *American Political Science Review* (December, 1958), pp. 1051-1066.
[4]Howard D. Hamilton *et. al.,* "Legislative Reapportionment," *Notre Dame Lawyer* (May, 1960), pp. 368-402.
[5]Murray Clark Havens, *City Versus Farm?* (University, Alabama: Bureau of Public Administration, University of Alabama, 1957).
[6]Malcolm E. Jewell, *The State Legislature, Politics and Practice* (New York: Random House, 1962), Ch. 3.

a tendency in this direction will ever be complete, but approaches to it may very well wipe out the ability of a substantial minority of the voters to provide a substantial legislative opposition party.

Surplus majorities which are requisite for the occurrence of the first of the above "frustrating conditions" may happen for any of several reasons. In the first place, they may be created deliberately by drawing district lines in such a way as to create large majorities for one party in some districts and small majorities for the other party in other districts. This is, of course, the essence of the gerry-mander. Surplus majorities may also be the product of demo-graphic trends which are manipulated by no one. For example, low income industrial workers may concentrate themselves in relatively few election districts producing huge majorities in those districts for the party which is favored by them. Majority bonuses are obviously also the result of demographic facts and not manipula-tion. There seems often to be some tendency in American politics for majority bonuses to occur since majority parties are often over-represented. Perhaps the most familiar instance is that elec-toral college majorities are often much larger than popular major-ities in presidential contests.

Several additional points may be made concerning surplus majorities and majority bonuses. First, they may appear when plurality voting systems are used, but would be less likely in a minority representation system. Second, surplus majorities and majority bonuses may occur in different combinations. Consider this situation: Party A usually has surplus majorities in a minority of the districts and the majority of districts are very closely con-tested in the aggregate. Party A when it wins will have surplus majorities and also a very large majority bonus. It will not be the governing party unless it gets well over 50 per cent of the votes. Party B may become the governing party with less than a majority of the votes by carrying the districts where a large majority bonus is possible and by failing to cut into the surplus majorities of Party A in the districts where A's strength is greatest; this is the first of the "frustrating conditions" referred to above.

Paradoxically, an election system may provide majority rule and minority representation despite substantial political inequality. For example, assume that Party A is city-based and that urban areas are under-represented. If Party A is able to win a large majority bonus in urban districts when it is the more popular party and if it wins some other seats, then it may very well be the governing party. What actually happens depends, of course, on the degree of rural over-representation and on the size of the majority bonus.

A good illustration of some of the things that have been said thus far and a good illustration of the potential complexities of an election system is furnished by consideration of the system the state of Ohio had in effect until the legislative elections of 1966. It is also an interesting system because it was successful by some of the usual tests.

The 1851 Constitution of Ohio included an election system that provided equal representation, periodic reapportionment, and effective barriers to gerrymandering.[7] Terms for members of the General Assembly were two years, and elections were to occur in odd-numbered years. Senate districts were formed by grouping the 88 counties of the state into 33 districts, and no county lines were crossed in forming senate districts. The population of the state was then divided by 35 in order to get a "ratio for a senator." Every district having a population at least equal to one-half of the ratio got one senator. Every district having one ratio and three-fourths over got two senators and so on. Districts with fractions above any ratio but less than three-fourths were entitled to an additional senator for one or more terms during a decennium depending on the size of the fraction. Districts with less than one-half of one ratio were to be attached to the least populous adjoining district. The combined districts would be represented according to their total population.

The Constitution provided for reapportionment of the Senate and the House every ten years beginning after the year 1851; hence, the first reapportionment was to be made in time for the fall 1861 elections. The governor, auditor, and secretary of state were made responsible for decennial reapportionment according to the plan given in the Constitution. They have never failed to do what was required.

Few changes in the system of electing senators have occurred between 1851 and 1966. One was a change to even rather than odd year elections that applied to all elective state offices and became

---

[7]*Constitution of Ohio,* Article XI.

effective in 1908. Another was a change to four year terms begun in 1958 and completed in 1960.

Representation in the House by the terms of the 1851 Constitution required division of the population of the state by 100 in order to find the "ratio of representation" in the House. Counties were then given representatives according to their population, and fractions were handled in the same way as for representation in the Senate. Counties with less than one-half of one ratio were to be attached to the least populous adjoining county, and the new district would be represented according to total population. Counties were not sub-districted. As a consequence some of the larger counties came to have sizeable at-large delegations. In recent years Cuyahoga County (Cleveland) elected as many as eighteen representatives at-large and Hamilton County (Cincinnati) elected nine.

A major change in the system was made in the fall of 1903 when the voters of the state approved a constitutional amendment to give every county at least one representative. The amendment is commonly known as the "Hanna Amendment," because of the part supposedly played by Mark Hanna in getting it adopted.

The principle criticism of the system was that rural areas were over-represented in the House, and this charge led to destruction of the system by the federal courts. The accusation was correct. In the mid-fifties, the eight largest urban counties in Ohio had within their borders 54 per cent of the state's population. They had 54 per cent of the seats in the Senate but only 39 per cent of the seats in the House.[8] Their deficit in the lower house was, therefore, 15 percentage points. Under the apportionment made effective in 1962, large urban counties had typically one representative for about every 80,000 people while some small counties with populations of ten or twelve thousand had one representative each as required by the Hanna amendment. In the period from 1947 through 1964, the eighteen counties classified as standard metropolitan areas or as parts of standard metropolitan areas had about two-thirds of the voters in elections for the House but only about one-half of the seats in that body.

But as indicated in an earlier argument, a districting system which lacks political equality nevertheless might provide majority

---

[8]The calculation is that of Gordon E. Baker, *Rural Versus Urban Political Power* (New York: Doubleday & Co., Inc., 1955), p. 16.

68

The Election System and the Party System
Flinn

rule and minority representation. To see if this might be the case in Ohio, House elections from 1948 to 1964 were analyzed. Data for each election were arranged as is shown in the table below which covers the elections of 1958 and 1962.

TABLE 3

Voters and Representation in the Ohio House, 1958 and 1962

	Metro Dems	Metro Reps	Non-Metro Dems	Non-Metro Reps
1958				
Voters	1,066,270	763,476	424,491	543,315
% of Metro or Non-Metro Voters	58.3	41.7	43.9	56.1
% of Metro or Non-Metro Seats	76.8	23.2	35.7	64.3
% of All Voters	38.1	27.3	15.2	19.4
Seats	53	16	25	45
% of All Seats	38.1	11.5	18.0	32.4
1962				
Voters	924,077	869,258	408,943	538,307
% of Metro or Non-Metro Voters	51.5	48.5	43.2	56.8
% of Metro or Non-Metro Seats	52.2	47.8	20.0	80.0
% of All Voters	33.7	31.7	14.9	19.6
Seats	35	32	14	56
% of All Seats	25.6	23.4	10.2	40.9

Legend: (1) Metropolitan voters are those living in counties classified as metropolitan by the Census Bureau, and non-metropolitan voters are those living in counties not classified as metropolitan.

(2) This table is based on voters, not votes. The reason is that in counties with more than one representative the voters are given a number of votes equal to the number of seats to be filled; so the number of votes cast will be considerably larger than the number of voters. In order to make the returns from the various counties comparable, it is necessary to consider the number of voters and not the number of votes. This is obtained by dividing

the number of votes cast in each county by the number
of seats to be filled. If it is the number of Democratic
and Republican voters in each county which is desired,
then the total number of votes cast for all Democratic
and for all Republican candidates is divided by the number of seats to be filled.

Notice that the Democrats got the support of 53.3 per cent of
the voters in 1958 (38.1 + 15.2) and got 56.1 per cent of the seats,
a good performance for any election system. The Democratic
majority in the House was produced by a large majority bonus in
the metropolitan counties that went to the Democrats and by
Democratic victories in about two dozen non-metropolitan counties. Notice that the Democrats had the support of 58.3 per cent
of the metropolitan voters but obtained 76.8 per cent of the metropolitan seats. Democratic and Republican voters had to be somewhat evenly distributed in the metropolitan constituencies, which
are, of course, counties. As a matter of fact, the Democratic or
Republican share of the votes in many metropolitan counties is
normally 50 per cent, give or take not more than about five percentage points. So when the trend is Democratic, many counties
pass over to that side and a counter movement occurs when
Republicans are doing well in the metropolitan counties, which is,
however, not so common. The likelihood of there being large
majority bonuses in the metropolitan counties was much enhanced
by the fact those counties were not sub-districted.

In 1962 the Republicans got the support of 51.3 per cent of the
voters (31.7 + 19.6) and got 64.3 per cent of the seats. Majority
rule was served; and although the majority party was substantially
over-represented, it seems fair to say adequate minority representation was provided also. In the metropolitan counties the Democrats did get a small majority, but it was so small that it produced
no significant majority.[9] In the non-metropolitan counties the

---

[9]In metropolitan counties the relation between per cent of voters and per cent
of seats was fairly regular during the period studied. The winning party got
for each percentage point above 50 per cent of the voters about 3.3 percentage
points of the seats above 50 per cent. Thus, a party getting the support of
58 per cent of the metropolitan voters would be expected to get 76 per cent of
the metropolitan seats (8 × 3.3 + 50) which is almost exactly what happened
in 1958. The election of 1962 was somewhat exceptional in that the expected
majority bonus did not appear. But it would not have changed the outcome.

Republicans had the support of 56.8 per cent of the voters and got 80 per cent of the seats, a very handsome majority bonus.

Majority rule was seemingly frustrated in two of the nine elections held in the period from and including 1948 and 1964. In 1948 the Democrats won 49.8 per cent of the voters but got 50.7 per cent of the seats in the House on the basis of a large majority bonus in the metropolitan counties. Actually, the Democrats could easily have had the backing of more than half of the voters if they had contested all the seats. They did not put up candidates in twenty-one non-metropolitan single-member districts while the Republicans defaulted in only two. In 1964 the Democrats got the support of 51.7 per cent of the voters, a clear but small majority, but got only 45.2 per cent of the seats. The election system had obviously reversed the outcome, although it certainly canceled no overwhelming mandate. The principal reason was that the expected majority bonus did not occur in the metropolitan counties. Instead the Democrats produced surplus majorities in some metropolitan counties while others were stubbornly refusing to follow the trend. But considering that the election system had usually served the cause of majority rule and minority representation, this one failure might be excused, especially since the election was, in fact, a close one conducted at the same time as a rather unusual national election. At any rate, so much for the Ohio experience. Some may wish to provide illustrations from other states.

In summary, election systems should provide political equality, majority rule, and minority representation. Political equality will probably carry with it the other two principles if the alternative governments are urban and rural factions; however, urban-rural factionalism is not characteristic of American state politics or, at least, does not exist in many states. Party competition is common, and it is rival parties which are the alternative governments. The question is then, "Does an election system that provides political equality also provide majority rule and minority representation when majority rule means that the party preferred by the largest number of people be given the chance to govern?" The answer is that it might, but "frustrating conditions" may intervene. Paradoxically, an election system may provide majority rule and minority representation even though there is considerable political inequality.

The conclusion is that either analysis or design of an election system is a complex task if it is to serve the principles that have been mentioned so often in this discussion: political equality, majority rule, and minority representation. Some place along the way the actual governing alternatives existing in the system must be properly identified. In American state politics these are frequently political parties, so the relation of the election system to the party system becomes crucial. This relation is likely to vary depending on how districts are drawn and how the supporters of each party are distributed among districts, and this too must be taken into account. It is actually possible under some circumstances to design a system with substantial virtues including majority rule and minority representation but without political equality. Some would certainly find such a system acceptable, and the writer is one.

The last comment is that judicial discussions of the operation of election systems show hardly any awareness of the complexity of the problem. The courts have indeed entered a thicket; yet one wonders whether the judges know the nature of the thicket. Some call it "political" meaning either that the problem is involved with political controversy or that there are no judicial standard to guide decision, whatever that may mean. Easily as troublesome is attaining adequate understanding of an election system in the context of an on-going political system. Perhaps this is too dim a view of the work of the courts, both judges and counsel. It may be that the courts can only emphasize political equality to the exclusion of equally important principles and cannot attempt to discover the realities of state politics for reasons which are perfectly good in a court of law. If this is true, then it is a powerful argument for judicial restraint.

Perhaps the analysis of election systems in context is best done by political scientists and the academic colleagues they can enlist. Some legislators will do their own political science, and it is hard to believe that the work of these academic and non-academic political scientists is going to be worse than the work of the judges and lawyers on the basis of present evidence. Decision might be left to elected officials. They may listen to whom they choose. Their decision is likely to reflect partisan advantage, attempted personal survival, and perhaps more general interests. Election systems will

The Election System and the Party System
Flinn

reflect their decision and what has happened with the passage of time to the distribution of population and to the distribution of party voters. Is that too bad, given the complexity of the problem and the need to deal with the genuine complexities of political life? The quick answer may be that no change is possible without judicial intervention, but the quicker response is that this is one of the least examined tenets in the dogma of the ardent reapportioner.

chapter eight

Some Observations in Ohio: Single-Member Districts, Multi-Member Districts, and the Floating Fraction

Howard D. Hamilton

The numerous proposals for constituting the Ohio Assembly are of three types: single-member districts plans, exemplified by the maps promulgated by the State Apportionment Board in October, 1965; multi-member district plans, exemplified by the much mooted idea of employing the new congressional districts for both chambers of the Assembly; and the floating-fraction system, which has prevailed since 1851, exemplified by the resolution enacted by the Senate last session.[1] That resolution was to restore the floating fraction to its pristine form, by setting .85 ratio as the minimum population of a district. The observations below are an effort to comprehend the operating effects of those three rival systems and to assess them as instruments of representation.

---

[1] Sub. S. J. R. No. 33, 106th General Assembly. A "ratio" is the mean number of constituents per senator or representative.

Criteria

These observations are grounded on the writer's notions of districting criteria. A researcher's criteria guide his work—one looks for what he thinks is significant. The following considerations are deemed fundamental:

1. *Equal representation* of people, the standard mandated by the Supreme Court.
2. *Equitable treatment of the parties.* A districting system ought to be neutral, not handicapping or benefiting either party, and it is good to the extent that the sizes of the party delegations in the Assembly correspond to the statewide election figures. Above all, a system should not produce minority party rule. Manifestly this standard rests on the premise that political parties are of some significance in state government.
3. *Competitive districts* in order to vitalize the party system and to maximize the legislature's sensitivity to the electorate.
4. A *districting mechanism* which is *automatic, objective,* and as *neutral* as possible so as to avoid the deliberate construction of safe districts and partisan gerrymandering.

Then at a lower level on the scale come:

5. The preservation of the territorial integrity of counties and cities.
6. The use of single-member districts in order to pinpoint responsibility and to make the legislator-constituent relationship as direct, visible, and strong as possible.

Manifestly no system could maximize all of those standards, because they collide frequently. Thus, single-member districts cannot exist universally without slicing up several counties and cities, and in Ohio the data below indicate that a universal single-member system conflicts with the goals of fairness to the political parties and responsible party government. Hence a system should be appraised in terms of all six considerations, with prime importance assigned to the standards of population equality, proportional representation of parties, party competition, and a neutral and scrupulously fair apportionment mechanism. Consequently the writer would be skeptical of a universal multi-district system (unless coupled with proportional representation as in Illinois), but some use of multi-member districts could produce important benefits to the total system.

Equalization Methods

Achievement of the first standard enumerated above and now a *sine qua non*, equal representation of people, requires some method of equalizing the number of constituents per legislator (not necessarily equally populated districts). Four methods of equalization are manifest in the apportionment systems across the nation: (1) the floaterial district superimposed on the regular districting pattern, (2) multi-member multi-county districts, (3) single-member districts which freely divide counties and cities, and (4) Ohio's floating fraction system, an ingenious device for attaining equal representation without dividing counties. None of the four methods appears to be entirely satisfactory; each has distinct weaknesses.

The floaterial district, superimposed on the regular districting pattern is inherently ambiguous, as Justices Clark and Harlan discovered in the Tennessee case.[2] As employed in the 1965 Indiana districting, it submerged the residents of some rural and suburban counties by attaching them to large urban counties, and it is a handy device for gerrymandering.[3]

The multi-member multi-county district is equally ambiguous and probably offers the maximum opportunity for gerrymandering. Almost innumerable combinations are possible, each affecting the fortunes of candidates and parties.

In most, or all, states single-member districts cannot achieve a modicum of equality without dividing counties and cities and crossing county lines rather frequently. Michigan has taken this road to equal representation. Its apportionment is the acme of population equality, but one may doubt whether the nearly perfect

---

[2] Justice Clark prorated by counties and found "a crazy quilt." Justice Harlan prorated by county populations and purported to perceive rationality in a sixty year old apportionment. *Baker v. Carr*, 369 U. S. 186 (1962).

[3] Ruled unconstitutional by a federal court for not affording equal representation. *Stout v. Bottorf*, 246 F. Supp. 825 (1965).

population equality was worth the cost when one looks at the district boundaries which snake through counties along township and municipal lines.

Drawing districts within counties and freely crossing county lines with visible guiding and constraining criteria can only engender endless controversy and widespread suspicion of gerrymandering. A computer could district without reference to county lines, aggregating wards and townships in an objective fashion. A legislature, or an apportionment agency composed of politicians, is unlikely to divide counties in utter disregard of all considerations but the census. Furthermore the computer can be programmed to achieve political objectives simultaneously with population equality.

The Floating Fraction

The Ohio constitutional "fathers" in 1851 were concerned about equal *and fair* representation. They devised a system to achieve four laudable objectives: population equality, regular reapportionment, a system which would be largely automatic with little room for discretion, and scant opportunity for gerrymandering. During the century of experience, the system has achieved three of their aspirations. The first objective, population equality, has been achieved for the Senate, within the concept of equalization over the decennium, but for the House that objective was vitiated by the "Hanna amendment" in 1903.

In 1962, Professors Schubert and Press applied sophisticated statistical techniques to measure the degree of population equality —and inequality—of the ninety-nine state legislative chambers and discovered that the Ohio Senate was one of the most equitably apportioned chambers in the nation, but the Ohio House ranked low.[4] If, however, the minimum House district were .85 ratio, as contemplated by the 1965 Senate resolution, the Ohio house would be a paragon of population equality, measured by any yardstick.[5]

[4]Glendon Schubert and Charles Press, "Malapportionment Remeasured," *American Political Science Review,* Dec. 1964, pp. 967-70. The Ohio Senate ranked third for the year 1962; but on a decennial basis it ranked first.
[5]Dauer-Kelsay index—percent of population to elect a majority of members (49%), per cent average deviation (3.2%), L/S ratio—largest/smallest district (1.38 to 1), inverse coefficient of variation (.95). The two chambers would have an S-P "apportionment score" of 108.4.

The floating fraction formula necessarily results in a few districts, those with a population between 1.2 and 2.0 ratio, which are conspicuously under-represented at one session and over-represented at the next session. For large districts the floating fraction variations are rather inconsequential. This poses a salient issue in current litigation. Is equalization over the decade "equal protection" or is it "substantially equal" representation? Patently the Ohio "fathers" thought it equitable and it was rarely questioned by their children until the recent litigation.

In appraisal of the four equalization methods, all achieve, or can achieve, very "substantial equality" of representation. The floating fraction, however, is free of defects inherent in the alternative devices which, lacking objective standards, are ambiguous, breed confusion and controversy, and permit gerrymandering. The single-member district device has the additional disadvantage of splitting up communities. The floating fraction standards have the objectivity and precision of mathematics, and their application is largely automatic with scant opportunity for gerrymandering. Objective, precise standards and automatic procedures are considerable virtues. Unless one rejects, in principle, the principle of equalization over a decennium, there is something to be said for the present formula.[6]

Multi-Member Districts

The disadvantage of the floating fraction have been mentioned. What are they? The sessional fluctuation, if it can be said to be inequitable at all, is not its major liability. Much more substantial are the defects accruing from constituencies with huge populations: the jungle ballot and the over-extended, obscured, and weakened bond between representative and constituents. If there is a correlation between size and the weight of the disadvantages of a multi-member district, some Ohio districts are not of optimal scale.

---

[6]Subsequent court decisions appear to bar further use of the floating fraction. A federal court ruled the device unconstitutional, and the case had been affirmed by the Supreme Court. See chapter VI.

Some Observations in Ohio: Single- Multi-Member Districts
Hamilton

This is not a blanket indictment of multi-member districts, which also have assets and in some situations may be superior to single-member districts. Also within a metropolis, single-member districts are likely to be artificial, nondescript areas, in which there is almost no medium of communication except direct canvassing of the voters.

One of the standard criticisms of multi-member districts—that they routinely produce a party sweep of all seats in the district, thereby distorting the *vox populi*—is less valid in Ohio than elsewhere. Assisted by the office block style ballot, Ohio voters in multi-member districts display extraordinary discrimination. Of the eighty-eight elections in multiple House districts since 1954, fifty-four were split decisions; only four (small) counties consistently put all their eggs in one party basket.

TABLE 1

Party Distribution of Seats
in Multi-member Districts of Ohio House

District	1954		1956		1958		1960		1962		1964	
	R	D	R	D	R	D	R	D	R	D	R	D
Butler	2	0	2	0	0	2	2	0	2	0	1	1
Columbiana	—		—		—		2	0	—		—	
Cuyahoga	1	16	2	16	0	18	1	16	2	15	0	17
Clark	—		2	0	2	0	—		—		—	
Franklin	6	0	6	0	3	3	7	0	7	0	6	1
Hamilton	9	0	9	0	6	3	8	1	8	1	6	3
Jefferson	—		—		—		0	2	—		—	
Lorain	1	1	1	1	0	2	0	2	0	2	0	2
Lucas	1	4	2	3	0	5	3	1	1	4	1	4
Mahoning	0	3	0	3	0	3	0	4	0	3	0	3
Montgomery	2	3	3	2	2	3	3	2	3	2	2	3
Stark	3	0	4	0	1	3	2	1	2	1	1	2
Summit	2	3	2	3	0	5	0	5	1	4	0	5
Trumbull	1	1	1	1	0	2	0	2	1	1	1	1
Total	28	31	34	29	14	47	28	36	27	33	18	42
SMD's	61	16	63	13	47	29	56	19	61	16	57	20
HOUSE	89	47	97	42	61	76	84	55	88	49	75	62

Source: *Ohio Election Statistics.*

Thus within nine of the thirteen districts there was some minority party representation, albeit hardly proportional. By contrast a single-member district provides no minority party representation. Also Table 1 shows that the sixty multi-member seats in the aggregate were distributed far more proportionately to the popular vote than seventy-seven single-member districts.

There is an important and easily overlooked consideration pertinent to the appraisal of multi-member districts: their influence on the total system. Table 1 shows that in 1956 the Republicans got most of the MMD seats; in 1954, 1960, 1962, each party got approximately the number of seats proportional to its popular vote in those thirteen counties; and in 1958 and 1964, the Democrats got more seats than their fraction of the popular vote. However, only in 1958 were the Democratic excess MMD seats equal to the Republican excess seats in the SMD districts.

Thus, the important effect of the MMD's has been occasionally and partially to offset the handicap of the Democrats in the SMD's. To phrase it more pointedly, only in 1958 was the number of "unrepresented" Republican voters in Cuyahoga equal to the number of "unrepresented" Democrats in the single-member districts of the state. The frequent proposal to "subdistrict" Cuyahoga for the benefit of those "unrepresented" Republicans is essentially a proposal to have more proportional representation in Cuyahoga while retaining the winner-take-all arrangement elsewhere. Proportional representation across the entire state, as in Illinois, has great merit, but on a selective basis it is a dubious thing.

TABLE 2

"Unrepresented" Voters: Ratio of Votes to Seats in Cuyahoga, Franklin, and Hamilton Counties

1000 Votes/Seat won	1954	1956	1958	1960	1962	1964
REP.	21.8	28.1	38.9	31.4	23.4	46.9
DEM.	20.0	27.1	19.0	31.8	25.6	31.9
Seats above party's pct. of votes	1 D	-0-	5 D	-0-	1 R	3 D

Derived from *Ohio Election Statistics.*

Perhaps because they are concentrated in one county, there is much lamentation about those "unrepresented" Cuyahoga Republican voters, but few tears for the usually greater number of "unrepresented" Democrats in the seventy-seven SMD's. There are also "unrepresented" Democrats in Franklin and Hamilton. In three of the last six elections the "unrepresented" Franklin and Hamilton Democrats equaled or exceeded the "unrepresented" Cuyahoga Republicans. Only in 1958 and 1964, did the Democrats gain more than a one seat advantage, and only in 1958 sufficient advantage to offset their disadvantage in the balance of the state.

Thus, it is evident that the multi-member districts, notably Cuyahoga, have had a compensating effect which has served to make the Ohio Assembly more representative partywise, although the effect usually has not been sufficient to offset the inequitable distribution of the seats partywise in the single-member districts. This suggests that a universal SMD pattern would be a strong handicap to the Democrats, possibly an insurmountable handicap. But let us first examine the congressional districts plan.

Congressional Districts as Legislative Districts

The effects of using the congressional districts for the Assembly, two senators and six representatives per district, would be determined by the characteristics of the congressional districts, which, of course, depends on how they were designed. In the author's view, one conspicuous characteristic of Ohio's congressional districts is their non-competitiveness partywise. A perusal of the election statistics for the past decade reveals that few districts appear to be competitive and many, impregnable. Although the number of strongholds now is slightly less, half of them remain solidly safe and in only three districts are the parties closely matched. This results in a state legislative pattern in which only one-eighth of the seats are competitive, where most of the seats will be impervious to political tides.[7]

---

[7]Paul T. David cites the tendency to create "safe" districts and to gerrymander. "There is a positive need for districting patterns that will promote competition between the parties rather than restrict it through the endless creation of safe seats. A genuinely competitive party system is not easily created despite the benefits it can confer on the electorate." *State Legislatures Progress Report,* Dec., 1965, p. 1.

TABLE 3

Political Complexion of Ohio Congressional Districts

	Old Districts	New Districts
Safe Dem.	9, 18, 19, 20, 21	9, 18, 20, 21
Democratic		3, 14, 16, 19
Marginal	1, 3, 10	1, 6, 13
Republican	13, 16, 17	7, 10, 12, 17, 24
Safe Rep.	2, 4, 5, 6, 7, 8, 11, 12, 14, 15, 22, 23	2, 4, 5, 8, 15, 11, 22, 23

Old districts classified by vote in recent elections.
New districts classified by vote for Repr. at Large, 1964.

Further findings indicate that Ohio congressional districts have been expertly designed to guarantee that most of the Ohio delegation will be Republicans. What the consequences would be for the state legislature is very predictable and can be measured by reference to the 1964 Congressman-at-Large vote within each of the new congressional districts. Using Congressman-at-Large data rather than the vote for Congressmen eliminates the extraneous influence of incumbency. The statewide popular vote of 47.85 per cent Republican and 52.15 per cent Democratic would have elected eighty Republicans and sixty Democrats. The same ratios would occur in the Senate, of course. The Ohio Assembly would be, in Al Smith's words, "constitutionally Republican." In the author's view these two characteristics of the congressional districts make it extremely difficult for authentic popular government to prevail.

Single-Member Districts: the SAB Models

Next consider the universal single-member district by examining the political consequences of the districts promulgated by the State Apportionment Board. It might be said that, in the light of current discussion, there is no way of knowing the political consequences of the SAB districts until the next election. However, given what

is known about political behavior,[8] it should be possible to make
some analysis, *if* a reliable and current index of the strength of

TABLE 4

Estimated Composition of Ohio Assembly Elected by
Congressional Districts (based on 1964 vote for Congr. at Large)

	1964 Vote C. at Large		If Popular Vote Reversed		If Popular Vote Equal	
	Rep.	Dem.	Rep.	Dem.	Rep.	Dem.
State vote	1,716,480	1,872,351	1,872,351	1,716,480	1,794,415	1,794,415
Pct.	47.85	52.15	52.15	47.85	50.00	50.00
Seats won						
House	84	60	102	42	96	48
Senate	28	20	34	14	32	16

the parties in each district can be located. In many states, such
indices are readily available (party enrollments or the vote for an
obscure state office whose duties and candidates are virtually
unknown to the electorate), but in Ohio the absence of party
enrollment and the office-block ballot generally impair efforts to
measure party strength. However, one recent election—for Congressman at Large in 1964—appears to be a rather good index
of party strength in Ohio.

The 1964 vote for Congressman-at-Large has been compiled for
each of the ninety-nine House and thirty-three Senate districts
and are presented in Appendix Table I and II. The aggregate vote
was 52.17 per cent Democratic and 47.83 per cent Republican
(in stark contrast to the 63 per cent 37 per cent ratio for the
Presidency). The tabulations indicate that had the SAB districts
been in effect the composition of the 106th Assembly would have
been eighteen Democrats and fifteen Republicans in the Senate
and a House of fifty-three Democrats and forty-six Republicans.[9]

---

[8]The vast research on voting behavior has informed us that American party
membership or attachment is rather stable and that swings of the electoral
pendulum tend to be of general scope geographically and sociologically. See
Burns and Peltason, *Government by the People,* 5th ed. (Englewood Cliffs,
N.J.: Prentice Hall, Inc, 1966), chap. 11.
[9]The actual 106th Assembly was a tied Senate and a House with a 75 to 62
Republican majority.

Tables I and II classify each of the districts in terms of its partisan character according to the size of the pluralities, as per Table 5.

TABLE 5

Classification System for SAB Districts Based on
Vote for Congressman at Large (1964 vote Adjusted)

Partisan Character		Size of Party Plurality in District	
		House	Senate
T	Toss up	0-999	0-2999
MD or MR	Marginal	1000-2999	3000-8999
SD or SR	Safe	3000-4999	9000-14999
SOD or SOR	Solid	5000 up	15000 up

Application of the Table 5 categories to the raw pluralities of the vote in the 1964 election might make Republican politicians unduly discouraged and give Democrats a false optimism. Consequently in Appendix Tables I and II, the 1964 vote has been adjusted, by converting it to a statewide ratio of 50.783 per cent Republican and 49.217 per cent Democratic, the mean of the last four elections. The Table 5 classification is applied to the resulting pluralities, with the results presented in Table 6, 7, and 8.

TABLE 6

Partisan Character of SAB Senate Districts

Solid Republican	1, 2, 7, 8, 16, 25, 31
Safe Republican	3, 14, 19, 26, 27, 32
Marginal Republican	6, 10, 13, 17
Toss up	4, 18
Marginal Democratic	12, 15, 20, 28, 29
Safe Democratic	5, 11, 21, 30, 33
Solid Democratic	9, 22, 23, 24

Source: Appendix Table I.

TABLE 7

Partisan Character of SAB House Districts

Solid Rep.	1, 4, 5, 6, 8, 14, 18, 23, 36, 37, 38, 49, 52, 54, 55, 56, 58, 65, 66, 67, 71, 73, 83, 84, 93
Safe Rep.	2, 11, 16, 19, 20, 24, 27, 29, 35, 62, 75, 76, 77, 94, 98
Marginal R.	3, 7, 10, 13, 15, 21, 26, 59, 68, 91, 99
Toss up	12, 17, 25, 28, 31, 34, 39, 40, 60, 61, 85, 86, 90, 92
Marginal D.	9, 22, 64
Safe Dem.	32, 43, 51, 53, 57, 70, 95, 96
Solid Dem.	30, 33, 41, 42, 44, 45, 46, 47, 48, 50, 63, 69, 72, 74, 78, 79, 80, 81, 82, 87, 88, 89, 97

Source: Appendix Table II.

TABLE 8

Partisan Character of SAB Districts

	Senate Districts			House Districts		
	Rep.	Dem.	Total	Rep.	Dem.	Total
Solid	7	4	11	25	23	48
Safe	6	5	11	15	8	23
Marginal	4	5	9	11	3	14
Toss up		2	2		14	14
	17	2 14	33	51 14	34	99

The results of the peregrinations to this point should be rather pleasing to those legislative candidates who win in Ohio in 1966. Most of the new incumbents can view the future with equanimity —unless the districts change again. But for one who postulates that a fundamental criterion for apportionment is competitive districts, Table 8 is a bit disconcerting; only two Senate and fourteen House districts are Toss Ups, two-thirds of the districts being Safe or Solid.

There are manifest parallels between the House and Senate data, as one would anticipate when three House districts constitute a Senate district, but there are also contrasts. In the Senate, the Democrats appear to have a three-seat handicap, but in the House a sixteen-seat handicap. The explanation of the Democrats' predicament in the House is not at all obscure: too many Solid districts.

Hence it would appear that in the Senate the Democrats have an uphill situation, but not a hopeless one. However, their future in the House looks rather bleak. Is the Democrats' predicament in the House the consequences of planning, or because their votes are distributed geographically in such a way that a single-member districts system inherently handicaps them?

Some light on these questions can be had by manipulating the index of party strength, the 1964 vote for Congressman at Large. In Tables 9 and 10 the results are ascertained for twelve different slicings of the total state vote, ranging from 45% D/55% R to 55% D/45% R (about the maximum amplitude of the pendulum of the state vote for the Assembly, although the vote for President or Governor has a greater amplitude).[10]

The data of Tables 9 and 10 are *muy interesante*. When the pendulum swings to a 45/55 distribution of the popular vote, the SAB districts system has about the same effect—short-changing the minority party (characteristic of a single-member districts system).

When the statewide vote draws closer, the SAB districts progressively benefit the Republican party. At the 50-50 mark the Republican party acquires a comfortable majority in the House and perhaps a working majority in the Senate. The Democrats must muster 51 per cent of the state vote to win a bare majority in the House and 52 per cent to get a one seat edge in the Senate.

Hence if the Democratic vote were in the range of 50 per cent to 52 per cent, minority rule would occur in one or both chambers. The state vote has not been within that interval during the past

---

[10]One reason for the shorter amplitude of the legislative vote shifts is that numerous Democratic voters attracted to the polls in a Presidential election never vote for lower echelon offices. The 1964 vote for Congressman at large ranged for 55 per cent of the population of the new 58th district to 20 per cent of the 48th district. An office block style ballot does have significant consequences.

Some Observations in Ohio: Single- Multi-Member Districts
Hamilton

decade, but in view of the 52.17 per cent Democratic vote in 1964, minority rule is a possibility endemic in the SAB districts.

TABLE 9

Estimated Composition of Senate Under SAB Districts, With Varying Distribution of Statewide Popular Vote

IF STATE VOTE—	1964 Vote in Reverse				Mean Last 4 Elections	
PCT. DEM.	45	47.83	48	49	49.217	49.5
SEATS WIN—						
DEM.	9	14	14	14	14	14
REP.	24	19	19	19	19	19
IF STATE VOTE—	Tie				1964 Vote	
PCT. DEM.	50	50.5	51	52	52.17	55
SEATS WIN—						
DEM.	15	16	16	17	18	23
REP.	18	17	17	16	15	10

TABLE 10

Estimated Composition of House Under SAB Districts, With Varying Distribution of Statewide Popular Vote

IF STATE VOTE—	1964 Vote in Reverse				Mean Last 4 Elections	
PCT. DEM.	45	47.83	48	49	49.217	49.5
SEATS WIN—						
DEM.	28	34	34	35	38	40
REP.	71	65	65	64	61	59
IF STATE VOTE—	Tie				1964 Vote	
PCT. DEM.	50	50.5	51	52	52.17	55
SEATS WIN—						
DEM.	45	49	50	52	53	66
REP.	54	50	49	47	46	33

Beyond the possibility of minority party rule, there is the inevitability of consistently unequal treatment of the parties. Observe the contrasting fortunes when a party garners 52 per cent of the popular vote.

TABLE 11

Seats Win with 52% of Popular Vote—SAB Districts

Popular Vote	Senate Seats (of 33)	House Seats (of 99)
If Rep. 52%	19 R	65 R
If Dem. 52%	17 D	52 D

Floating Fraction Also Discriminates

This analysis indicates that in Ohio a universal single-member district system does not operate in a neutral fashion. Furthermore the evidence indicates that Republicans have benefited more often than Democrats. Such is largely due to the facts of political demography—the Democratic votes are insufficiently scattered over Ohio, resulting in a disproportionate volume of "wasted votes."

This suggests a new query. Would that political demography have the effect of making the Floating Fraction System operate to the advantage of the Democrats and to the detriment of the Republicans? Truly, the FFS is admirably neutral as a formula for apportioning seats to attain population equality in the districts, but is its operation neutral partywise? Also, it appears that recent elections have frequently short-changed the Democrats in the Ohio House, but that was because of the "Hanna amendment." How would the FFS operate partywise in an era of equal representation?

To test this hypothesis, the House has been "districted" (easy in the privacy of one's study) in accordance with Sub. S.J.R. No. 33, using a divisor of 100 and .85 ratio as the minimum district population, achieving distinctly greater equality of district populations than the SAB districts (an average deviation of 3.0 per cent compared to 6.3 per cent). The political effects of that map have been analyzed by repeating the computer runs that were used for the SAB districts, estimating the composition of the House with twelve different slicings of the statewide popular vote.

TABLE 12

Estimated Composition of House Under Floating Fraction System, With Varying Distribution of Statewide Popular Vote

IF STATE VOTE—	1964 Vote in Reverse			Mean Last 4 Elections		
PCT. DEM.	45	47.83	48	49	49.217	49.5
SEATS WIN—						
DEM.	6	36	41	48	49	51
REP.	93	63	58	51	50	48
IF STATE VOTE—	Tie				1964 Vote	
PCT. DEM.	50	50.5	51	52	52.17	55
SEATS WIN—						
DEM.	51	53	54	57	68	82
REP.	48	46	45	42	31	17

The results, presented in Table 12, certainly resemble the analysis of the SAB districts (Table 10) but reversed partywise, although not an identical image. With a 50/50 state popular vote, the Democrats rather than the Republicans have a three seat plurality. To gain a majority, the Republicans would require close to 51 per cent of the popular vote. The probability of minority party rule appears to be rather lower.

Which system operationally discriminates the most? Extracting from Tables 10 and 12, we get the answer of Table 13. When the majority party vote exceeds 52 per cent, the Democrats as the majority have a greater advantage under the FFS than accrues to the Republicans as the majority under the SAB districts. At three intervals in Table 13, the two systems discriminate the same amount, but at five intervals the advantage of the Republicans under the SAB districts is distinctly greater than the corresponding advantage of the Democrats under the floating fraction system. Conclusion: Neither system is neutral in operation vis-à-vis the parties; both discriminate in a similar fashion—one for the Elephant, the other for the Donkey—but the floating fraction system discriminates less.

TABLE 13

Which System Discriminates the Most?

IF STATE VOTE— OF MINORITY PARTY	45%	47.83%	48%	49.217%	49.5%
SEATS WIN—					
DEM.-Fl. Fr. Sy.	6	36	48	49	51
REP.-SAB Sy.	33	46	49	49	50
IF STATE VOTE— OF MAJORITY PARTY	50%	50.5%	51%	52%	55%
SEATS WIN—					
DEM.-Fl. Fr. Sy.	51	53	54	68	82
REP.-SAB Sy.	54	59	64	65	71

An Adaptation of the German Hybrid?

Could there be a universal single-member district system which operates neutrally vis-à-vis the parties? Evidently not in Ohio with the SAB districts, and certainly not if the districts were subtly gerrymandered. But yes, if Ohio would link to the single-member district system some scheme of proportional representation, like the hybrid of the German Federal Republic.

The essence of the German system is that half of the Bundestag members are elected by simple plurality in single-member districts, the other half from party lists in each state. The German votes for his district deputy and also for a party list. His *Erststimme* is his choice of personality; his *Zweitstimme* is his choice of party, which of course may not be parallel. The results of the *Zweitstimmen* determine each party's share of the total seats, from which is subtracted the single-member districts won on the *Erststimmen*, and its deficit is filled from the party list. Thus the German can vote for "the good man" to be his deputy without being obliged to vote against his party—a felicitous accommodation of the legitimate claims of personality and party.

Two manifest drawbacks of the German system, beyond being "foreign," are that two few of the seats are single-member districts and there is no handy instrument for nominating the party list. The latter problem, might be solved by permitting each party caucus in the legislature to coöpt its increment. Then the proportion of single-member seats in a chamber could be more than half by authorizing only the minority caucus to coöpt members sufficient to achieve its proportional seats. Thus, the aggregate membership of a chamber would oscillate each legislature, a phenomenon which may be quite feasible and no novelty in Ohio.

An important bonus of such a system would be its cure of gerrymandering. One would anticipate little gerrymandering with the profit eliminated, and if any occurred the victimized party would be automatically compensated. The writer does not recommend (nor oppose) such a "foreign system"; it is merely mentioned for the benefit of those who might be enamored by single-member districts, but who also feel that party government and elemental justice require proportional representation.

Conclusion

The preceding reference to gerrymandering and the earlier stipulation of no gerrymandering as a fundamental criterion leads to a postscript. If the floating fraction system were abandoned, gerrymandering would be possible, and Ohio voters should give attention to what—or who—shall be the districting agency. In this respect Ohio has been a pace-setter of the country by about a century, having wisely, in the writer's judgment, divested the legislature of the districting function in favor of its rather automatic and objective system. Without the floating fraction, the door is open to gerrymandering, which can be readily, sometimes subtly, done within a framework of equally populated districts.

APPENDIX TABLE I

Political Character of Ohio Senate Districts

Promulgated by State Apportionment Board, Oct. 15, 1965

Senate District	1964 Vote Congressman at Large			If State Vote 50.783% R (Mean of last four elections)			Partisan Character
	R	D	R Plurality	R	D	R Plurality	
1	60271	49061	11210	63049	46282	16766	SOR
2	65352	52195	13157	68307	49239	19068	SOR
3	56916	56963	−47	60141	53737	6404	MR
4	52538	58472	−5934	55849	55160	688	T
5	40854	57617	−16763	44116	54354	−10237	SD
6	54478	54145	333	57544	51078	6465	MR
7	66175	53973	12202	69231	50916	18314	SOR
8	74574	61379	13195	78049	57903	20146	SOR
9	24765	50289	−25524	27612	47441	−19828	SOD
10	55667	53035	2632	58670	50031	8638	MR
11	42068	59582	−17514	45442	56207	−10765	SD
12	47987	57646	−9659	51251	54381	−3130	MD
13	53062	50145	2917	55901	47305	8596	MR
14	66683	59058	7625	70027	55713	14313	SR
15	38644	50666	−12022	41513	47796	−6283	MD
16	74797	50193	24604	77639	47350	30288	SOR
17	50969	52794	−1825	53958	49804	4154	MR
18	47221	51490	−4269	50136	48574	1562	T
19	49542	42610	6932	51955	40196	11758	SR
20	51261	66771	−15510	55042	62989	−7947	MD
21	34999	54115	−19116	38063	51050	−12986	SD
22	26766	65673	−38907	30485	61953	−31468	SOD
23	21454	50986	−29532	24341	48098	−23757	SOD
24	57736	83959	−26223	62490	79204	−16713	SOD
25	68585	58106	10479	71875	54815	17060	SOR
26	70076	62889	7187	73637	59327	14309	SR
27	61858	58240	3618	65156	54941	10214	SR
28	47797	60189	−12392	51205	56780	−5574	MD
29	43949	57365	−13416	47197	54116	−6918	MD
30	45744	68472	−22728	49621	64594	−14972	SD
31	63793	45831	17962	66388	43235	23152	SOR
32	55665	50882	4783	58546	48000	10545	SR

Some Observations in Ohio: Single- Multi-Member Districts
Hamilton

APPENDIX TABLE I (Con't.)

Senate Dis- trict	1964 Vote Congressman at Large			If State Vote 50.783% R (Mean of last four elections)			Par- tisan Char- acter
	R	D	R Plurality	R	D	R Plurality	
33	43411	62978	−19567	46977	59411	−12434	SD
State	1716480	1872351		1822511	1766320		

SOR	Solid Republican	SOD	Solid Democratic
SR	Safe Republican	SD	Safe Democratic
MR	Marginal Republican	MD	Marginal Democratic

T Toss Up

APPENDIX TABLE II

Political Character of Ohio House Districts

Promulgated by State Apportionment Board, Oct. 15, 1965

House District	1964 Vote Congressman at Large			If State Vote 50.783% R (Mean of last four elections)			Partisan Character
	R	D	R Plurality	R	D	R Plurality	
1	19875	15485	4390	20751	14608	6143	SOR
2	20531	18330	2201	21569	17291	4277	SR
3	20179	21587	−1408	21401	20364	1036	MR
4	21164	16080	5084	22074	15169	6905	SOR
5	24373	18439	5934	25417	17394	8022	SOR
6	20448	15426	5022	21321	14552	6769	SOR
7	22365	21956	409	23608	20712	2895	MR
8	20237	16356	3881	21163	15429	5733	SOR
9	14314	18651	−4337	15370	17594	−2224	MD
10	16746	16792	−46	17696	15841	1855	MR
11	17716	15255	2461	18579	14391	4188	SR
12	17731	19236	−1505	18820	18146	673	T
13	18077	18336	−259	19115	17297	1817	MR
14	19103	15747	3356	19994	14855	5139	SOR
15	21341	20748	593	22515	19573	2942	MR
16	22218	19681	2537	23332	18566	4766	SR
17	15419	17301	−1882	16398	16321	77	T
18	25545	21546	3999	26765	20325	6439	SOR
19	18920	17831	1089	19929	16821	3108	SR
20	20220	18544	1676	21270	17493	3776	SR
21	15297	14042	1255	16092	13246	2845	MR
22	17072	22473	−5401	18344	21200	−2855	MD
23	20481	14982	5499	21329	14133	7195	SOR
24	15400	12160	3240	16088	11471	4617	SR
25	18285	19566	−1281	19393	18457	935	T
26	13894	14239	−345	14700	13432	1267	MR
27	16255	14778	1477	17091	13941	3150	SR
28	19563	21858	−2295	20800	20620	180	T
29	19603	18259	1344	20637	17224	3412	SR
30	12095	26654	−14559	13604	25144	−11540	SOD
31	13661	15468	−1807	14536	14592	−55	T
32	13693	20203	−6510	14837	19058	−4221	SD
33	13037	26635	−13598	14545	25126	−10581	SOD

Some Observations in Ohio: Single- Multi-Member Districts
Hamilton

APPENDIX TABLE II (Con't.)

House District	1964 Vote Congressman at Large			If State Vote 50.783% R (Mean of last four elections)			Partisan Character
	R	D	R Plurality	R	D	R Plurality	
34	19014	21634	−2620	20239	20408	−169	T
35	18154	15269	2885	19018	14404	4614	SR
36	22587	13438	9149	23347	12677	10670	SOR
37	23052	17124	5928	24021	16154	7867	SOR
38	19580	16391	3189	20508	15462	5045	SOR
39	14698	16811	−2113	15650	15858	−208	T
40	17661	20074	−2413	18797	18937	−139	T
41	5651	18823	−13172	6716	17757	−11040	SOD
42	4219	16873	−12654	5174	15917	−10742	SOD
43	9919	16805	−6886	10870	15853	−4982	SD
44	7851	25083	−17232	9271	23662	−14391	SOD
45	8996	23785	−14789	10342	22438	−12095	SOD
46	3563	13546	−9983	4330	12778	−8448	SOD
47	13381	23555	−10174	14714	22221	−7506	SOD
48	4510	13885	−9375	5296	13098	−7802	SOD
49	21120	17870	3250	22131	16858	5273	SOR
50	18213	30864	−12651	19960	29116	−9155	SOD
51	19022	26129	−7107	20501	24649	−4147	SD
52	34268	18109	16159	35293	17083	18210	SOR
53	16377	21997	−5620	17622	20751	−3128	SD
54	25129	18419	6710	26172	17375	8796	SOR
55	24785	22246	2539	26044	20986	5058	SOR
56	28914	18646	10268	29969	17590	12379	SOR
57	20501	26966	−6465	22028	25438	−3410	SD
58	43592	19347	24245	44687	18251	26436	SOR
59	18138	17635	503	19136	16636	2500	MR
60	17387	19186	−1799	18473	18099	374	T
61	16739	18360	−1621	17778	17320	458	T
62	14466	12486	1980	15173	11778	3394	SR
63	6150	15293	−9143	7016	14426	−7410	SOD
64	14356	17738	−3382	15360	16733	−1372	MD
65	21424	18178	3246	22453	17148	5304	SOR
66	23410	18790	4620	24474	17725	6748	SOR
67	21341	17005	4336	22303	16042	6261	SOR
68	20517	19983	534	21648	18851	2797	MR
69	5554	17220	−11666	6529	16244	−9715	SOD

APPENDIX TABLE II (Con't.)

House District	1964 Vote Congressman at Large			If State Vote 50.783% R (Mean of last four elections)			Partisan Character
	R	D	R Plurality	R	D	R Plurality	
70	13768	19029	−5261	14845	17951	−3105	SD
71	24980	19645	5335	26092	18532	7559	SOR
72	5443	14040	−8597	6238	13244	−7006	SOD
73	29077	21751	7326	30308	20519	9789	SOR
74	13197	22127	−8930	14450	20873	−6423	SOD
75	18540	17097	1443	19508	16128	3379	SR
76	19232	17496	1736	20222	16505	3717	SR
77	22974	21020	1954	24164	19829	4334	SR
78	10081	18872	−8791	11149	17803	−6653	SOD
79	9013	19690	−10677	10128	18574	−8446	SOD
80	8569	18562	−9993	9620	17510	−7890	SOD
81	14806	23689	−8883	16147	22347	−6199	SOD
82	7529	21888	−14359	8768	20648	−11879	SOD
83	21076	17401	3675	22061	16415	5645	SOR
84	26531	18682	7849	27588	17624	9964	SOR
85	15543	16946	−1403	16502	15986	516	T
86	17121	18888	−1767	18190	17818	372	T
87	9777	17053	−7276	10742	16087	−5344	SOD
88	6766	20165	−13399	7907	19023	−11115	SOD
89	11337	21070	−9733	12530	19876	−7346	SOD
90	14117	15526	−1409	14996	14646	349	T
91	20453	19764	689	21572	18644	2927	MR
92	18495	20769	−2274	19671	19592	78	T
93	27242	20253	6989	28388	19106	9282	SOR
94	22316	19741	2575	23433	18623	4810	SR
95	15044	22179	−7135	16299	20923	−4623	SD
96	12300	18246	−5946	13333	17212	−3879	SD
97	11511	22051	−10540	12759	20802	−8042	SOD
98	17922	15409	2513	18794	14536	4258	SR
99	18163	19082	−919	19243	18001	1242	MR

State 1716480 1872351   1822511 1766320

SOR	Solid Republican	SOD	Solid Democratic
SR	Safe Republican	SD	Safe Democratic
MR	Marginal Republican	MD	Marginal Democratic

T   Toss Up

chapter nine

Computer Methods of Districting

Myron Q. Hale

Introduction

The continuing problem of democratic government is motivating popular participation in the formulation of public policy. Speaking historically, "direct" and "representative" were the two forms of political democracy proposed as alternatives. Since direct democracy was impossible beyond the village, in industrial societies the accepted form became representative democracy with the emphasis on suffrage. It was hoped that universal and equal suffrage could implement the important values of popular participation and the responsibility of the rulers to the ruled. While suffrage did not exhaust the necessary procedures, it was doubted that a representative democracy could exist without equal participation in the choice of leaders.

The foremost concern of democratic movements from the seventeenth through the first part of the twentieth century was their demand for equal participation in government through "political" representation based on one person-one vote. From the Chartist movement through the political struggles of European social democrats, the center of the conflict was the extension of the suffrage and the gradual abolition of inequalities. In view of the predominant position of suffrage in the history of democratic movements, it is surprising that so little is written on the subject.

The idea of a system of "political" representation based on the principle of political equality of the citizens regardless of their economic power or their social standing was challenged about the middle of the nineteenth century. While the critique became widespread, the most significant came from two sides, i.e., Marxists and traditionalists.

The Marxists' criticism was based on the argument that in bourgeois societies political equality alone is a "sham." As long as economic and social power relationships prevail a dictatorship of the ruling class will exist under the guise of political equality. Prior to the establishment of a workable political democracy, according to them, the social and economic system need revamping to eliminate the economic and social power of the few over the many.

The traditionalists denied that representative democracy based on "political" representation was possible, since it relied on a false premise, i.e., the principle of abstract individualism in which the citizen is conceived as an isolated individual allegedly participating in the formation of public policy. For the traditionalists, the citizen was not an isolated individual, but rather was active within specific social and economic organizations primarily determined by his relation to the process of production. Representation, therefore, must be based on the citizen's status in society. From this position various ideological trends evolved, but the traditionalist, along with others, advocated substituting functional or corporate representation for "political" representation.

The argument over representation is not settled, but has taken various forms. It seems clear, however, that representation that is equal is looked upon as legitimate.[1] And the link between representation and legitimacy is the responsibility of the rulers to the ruled through a system of free elections. Just as "political" representation without voters had no meaning, voting without free choice cannot result in representative government. In order that the followers may exercise restraint, influence, and control over leaders, they must have the power to choose them.

---

[1]See Carl J. Friedrich, *Man and His Government: An Empirical Theory of Politics* (New York: McGraw-Hill, 1963), pp. 301-314.

Those who defend a system of equal representation through one person—one vote emphasize the dynamic nature of representative democracy. Changes can be "rationally" carried out by the leaders with the absence of open warfare. In fact, the very justification of a democratic political system is based not on the idea of inevitable violence or a closed society resulting in social paralysis, but on the belief that peaceful transition from one to another social system is possible.

While there are obvious exceptions, speaking generally, the attainment of universal suffrage dates from approximately the first quarter to the middle of the twentieth century. The principle of political equality, understood in the sense that every man counts for one vote, and that one man's vote is the equivalent of the next man's, has been accepted. But even with equal suffrage iniquities exist, in part, because of "gerrymandering"—except in those instances where there is strict proportional representation. Gerrymandering takes different forms but the most prevalent in the United States has been "silent" gerrymandering, i.e., the refusal of legislative bodies to redistrict or reapportion following significant population shifts.

In part, the failure to redistrict was due to the division of the country into electoral districts antedating the rise of industrial society and the ensuing struggle which developed in the legislatures between rural and urban representatives. While there were many additional reasons for the urban-rural conflict, silent gerrymandering became a persistent and prevailing phenomenon. It not only gives preference to agrarian over industrial interests, but it has an impact on the political structure of the state in that it undermines the prospect of greater participation through party competition.

The urban-rural conflict in the form of silent gerrymandering delineated the difficult problems of reapportioning and redistricting. Legislators look upon redistricting as a form of redistributive policy, i.e., shifts in political power are inevitable when existing political boundaries are altered. They are keenly aware that neutral redistricting systems are nonexistent—once you have drawn lines on a map it becomes easier for some people to get elected than others. Districts are the focal points of political conflict, since the power structure perceives any change in the representational pattern as a change in the balance of political power.

The study of representation in legislative bodies received unprecedented stimulation following the "reapportionment" decisions of the U.S. Supreme Court. From these decisions one thing is clear: districting and apportioning must not be according to a geographic-population combination, but in terms of one theory of representation—equal population.[2]

In drawing equal population districts or constituencies by computer, just as in the establishment of any political boundary, the essential questions relate to the organization of power in the political system. How is the distribution of power in the legislature likely to be affected by the varying computer districting arrangements? Who is more likely to gain by the use of a particular computer program? Who gains by another pattern? More is involved than the choice of the computer method, for certain interests may be consistently favored in one program and slighted in another. These interests, moreover, represent particular types of values and ideology. Certain values are much more characteristic of one type of computer program, and other values more readily given expression and support in another type of computer program. Since computer programs explicitly or implicitly promote particular values, once political judgments have been made, computer utilization becomes possible. Computers will help, but they are not machines to grind the political judgments out of districting.

Computers: How Far Will They Take Us?

The U.S. Supreme Court's equal population principle gave birth to the use of computers for redistricting purposes. The idea of districting by computer gained support as more legislatures entered the "political thicket" which Justice Frankfurter had warned his colleagues on the Court to avoid. It was suggested that the computer could "mow-down" the political thicket and that state legislatures could comply with the Court's one man—one vote

---

[2]While the Court has not outright rejected other criteria such as political subdivisions, history, economic or other group interests, geographical considerations, natural boundary lines, area, size of districts, representation for sparsely settled areas, and occupation, none of them alone provide sufficient justification for deviations from the equal-population principle.

order. Not only could the computer solve the immediate redistricting problems of the various states, but William Boyd of the National Municipal League predicted that in fifty years computers will do all redistricting, and that an overwhelming majority of states will take redistricting out of the hands of legislatures and turn it over to special commissions. This may prove to be the case, since the problem of reapportioning and redistricting handled by legislators grows from a thicket into a jungle.

Immediately following the Supreme Court's decision in *Baker v. Carr*, 1962, the Committee of 39, a nonpartisan Wilmington, Delaware group, began gathering statistics and apportionment information on all states. The Committee wanted a rapid, nonpartisan method of districting. A team of five organization and research analysts and engineers announced the development of a computer method based on the familiar criteria: equal population, contiguity, and compactness.[3] James B. Weaver, Chairman of the Committee of 39's Reapportionment Committee, proposed using the computer as a tool to carry out redistricting on a nonpartisan basis. Dr. Sidney W. Hess suggested the computer method based upon the approach industry takes in locating warehouses to minimize the cost of sending freight to customers. CROND'S (Computer Research on Nonpartisan Districting) immediate goals, according to Weaver and Hess, are to investigate various techniques advanced for nonpartisan districting, to improve their technique, and to serve as a general information center about using computers to establish voting districts. By 1970 CROND'S goal is an easy to use, documented, accepted, nonpartisan method for legislative districting.

Because of the attention given to the use of electronic computers and the Weaver-Hess method, and as a means of speeding up state reapportioning and redistricting, the Committee on Continuing Legal Education of the American Law Institute and the American Bar Association (ALI-ABA) held a seminar in Washington, D. C., in October, 1965. The "ALI-ABA Conference on Computers in Redistricting" explored the status of legislation and litigation,

---

[3]The five Delawareans were awarded a $96,000 Ford Foundation grant to perfect for nationwide use computer redistricting techniques to be developed by 1970. The grant was made through the National Municipal League and was part of a $900,000 study that group is making of reapportionment developments.

criteria for districting, problems in data, courtroom presentation, and implementation of computer districts.

The Conference reached the conclusion that there must be discussion and decisions on criteria in legislative apportionment, i.e., single-member or multi-member districts; on the use of existing political boundaries; on whether districts must be homogenous or heterogenous; on partisan dominance or "fairness"; on protection of incumbents; and on allowance of maximum variance between district population, *inter alia*. A second conclusion was that although everyone accepted the idea that equal population was a starting point, the equal population-compactness-contiguity concepts were inadequate. Contiguity could be mishandled, and compactness has not been adequately defined.[4]

A third conclusion reached at the ALI-ABA Conference was that computers can help immeasurably in apportionment, in speed and accuracy. Under certain circumstances they can create almost "perfect apportionment" or they can be used in the worst way for gerrymandering. The computer limitation is in the human element. The computer must be programmed with criteria on which the districting will be based.

Computer Programs For Districting

Among other things, the capabilities of the computer include speed, the ability to recognize certain conditions and take appropriate action as a result, to manipulate symbols, to follow each detailed instruction in idiot-like fashion, and by a suitable combination of detailed steps, to be programmed to exhibit intelligent behavior. Communicating with a computer involves a program in detailed procedural "machine" language. The computational task is normally expressed in a "high-level" language. If the "high-level"

---

[4]Contiguity can readily lend itself to gerrymandering, for there could be a long "ribbon" district which would be contiguous yet would assure domination by one political party. Compactness should refer to a shape which has a minimum perimeter for a given area, a more or less round or square district. Yet this shape might interfere with city, town or county boundaries, which might be rivers, mountains, or other natural lines.

language is unambiguous, the computer itself can perform the translation from high-level language into machine language.[5]

A problem to be solved must be expressed in the form of a model which will include controllable and non-controllable variables, functional relationships, and criteria for comparing alternatives, e.g., redistricting plans may be compared on the basis of compactness, contiguity, population distribution, relation to existing districts, partitioning of communities, etc. Computers can optimize: draw districts that maximize a certain factor or a weighted combination of factors—population, compactness, political strength, preservation of incumbents, etc.—which are specified in advance. A computer can produce a number of acceptable solutions within a given range of variations, and some computer programs will yield a single best, "unique" solution. An optimizing model finds the "unique" solution in terms of a specific criterion of effectiveness. Computers can simulate: determine the characteristics of any number of district plans already drawn, showing the likelihood in party strength, etc., for each. A simulated model merely determines the consequences of a specified alternative.

Computers can play an important role not only in districting, but in the testing and suggesting of alternative redistricting plans, provided the data are sufficiently detailed and the parameters (instructions) are sufficiently varied. A number of different computer districting programs have been developed, but a basic question remains: what criteria should be considered in the attempt to implement one of the programs which operationalize "equal" representation? Drawing lines on a map will advantage some people and disadvantage others.

Decisions on what criteria should be used for districting by computer are political judgments. Since the computer will draw district lines in accord with the criteria written into the particular program, political judgments should be built into the model. In this way value judgments can be made explicit. Although there are significant differences among them, most computer programs developed so far have tried to maximize population equality while maintaining contiguity and compactness, and minimizing or ignoring other factors. This may be one of the reasons that some state

---

[5]See "The Computer as a Problem-Solving Tool," a paper delivered by Dr. James C. Emery at the "ALI-ABA Conference on Computers in Redistricting," Washington, D. C., Oct. 22-23, 1965.

legislatures have not been anxious to see computers used in redistricting.

Computer districting techniques are in various stages of development. The Weaver-Hess method (CROND) is analogous to the "warehouse-location" problem. "Diminishing fractions mapping," a second technique advanced by Forrest, develops rectangular or square districts by successively dividing an area in halves. The OSU method creates "wedge-shaped" districts about a circular district centered on the population centroid. A fourth program, the Kaiser-Nagel method, attempts to improve old districts by moving each exterior population unit into an adjacent district or by swapping it with one in another district.

The Weaver-Hess Method

According to CROND, their computer method is nonpartisan and designed to produce districts that are compact, contiguous and as equal in population as possible. While the method was used to draft a plan for redistricting the General Assembly of Delaware, the main emphasis is on perfecting the program. The Weaver-Hess method utilizes an industry technique used to locate warehouses close to the center of demand in sales territories. The program locates a specific number of warehouses (district centers) and assigns customers (population units) to each warehouse. Total freight cost of assignment (sum of squared distances between each person and his district center) is to be minimized. This is districting by minimizing the amount of inertia. Warehouse capacities (district populations) must be nearly equal. The latter restriction and the known number of districts are specific to the districting problem, but not to the warehouse-location problem.

Since the districts are formed around concentrations of populations, Weaver and Hess believe their method eliminates the possibility of gerrymandering and enhances the prospect of a district's population having a common interest.

Our principle was to center the districts in general on the center of population. We wrapped the districts around the cities rather than setting them up so that part of a city could go to two districts. The actual measure used to do this minimizes the distance each individual is from the center of his final legislative district. This tends to make compact geographic units but it's really calculated on a population measure.[6]

By developing a computer districting program which places greatest emphasis on compactness—at the same time drawing districts with a given population range—their plan tends to provide symmetrical districts. But because Weaver and Hess are attempting to reflect at least to some extent popular interests in districting and because population patterns may coincide with interest patterns, the principle of compactness is defined as a measure of population as well as geographic concentration. Under this definition a district's boundaries will not necessarily approach a circle as a limit as greater compactness is achieved. But constructing districts using this compactness definition will tend to locate districts of maximum compactness around centers of population, whereas, under prior definitions, compact districts would as likely divide population centers as respect them.

Application of the Weaver-Hess definition of compactness would tend to discourage districts of extremely elongated shapes, since the farther a part of the district is from the population center of that district, the more it will add to the moment of inertia. Similarly, it would tend to create districts the population centers of which coincide with areas of high population density, since the closer that high density area is to the population center of its district, the smaller will be the distance squared factor by which the population figure will be multiplied, and consequently the lower will be the moment of inertia. Since it is the sum of these moments of inertia of each district in the plan which is minimized, these phenomena are tendencies and not certainties.

The "enumeration district," the smallest unit of population count provided by the United States Census, was chosen as the minimum unit in the Weaver-Hess program. Averaging under 1,000 in population, the enumeration district has natural boundaries of the type usually desired for "legislative districts," such as rivers, highways, or railroads. Legislative districts will generally be suffi-

[6]James B. Weaver and Sidney W. Hess, "A Procedure for Nonpartisan Districting: Development of Computer Techniques," *The Yale Law Review,* Vol. 73 (December, 1963), 288-308. The material in this section is taken from this article. But see in addition, James B. Weaver and Sidney W. Hess, "Districting by Machine," *National Civic Review,* 53 (1964), p. 293.

ciently large in population to permit quite precise equalization of population even though each enumeration district must be wholly contained within a legislative district. Since census data do not establish the location of individuals within each enumeration district, all people are assumed to be located at the geographic center of their respective enumeration district. The chosen measure of compactness makes it possible to take advantage of certain mathematical similarities between the redistricting problem and a problem already programmed on computers—that of assigning customer orders to specific warehouse locations so as to minimize freight costs. This program, supplemented for this specific use by various additional steps and subcalculations, assigns "enumeration districts" (customers) to "legislative districts" (warehouses) in a manner minimizing moment of inertia (freight cost.)[7]

It is necessary to make a set of initial guesses as to the population centers of each legislative district (warehouse location), and then to feed the coordinates of those guesses into the computer. The computer assigns each enumeration district to a legislative district in a way that minimizes the sum of the moments of inertia about the hypothesized centers for the entire unit being districted. A characteristic of the existing program requires exactly equal population in the legislative districts; therefore, the computer generally will assign parts of one or more enumeration districts to different legislative districts. To counteract this phenomenon, a supplementary computer program reunites split enumeration districts so that the *entire enumeration district* is assigned the legislative district having the largest share of the enumeration district's population. Based on this reassignment, the computer then calculates the population and moment of inertia of each legislative district and totals the moment of inertia of the entire unit districted. This procedure is continued until no change in enumeration district assignment results from the use of calculated as opposed to trial legislative district centers.[8]

---

[7] Since districting by minimizing the moment of inertia involves numerous calculations, application of this procedure by hand would require considerable time and introduce significant probability of arithmetic error, according to Weaver and Hess.

[8] According to Weaver and Hess, there is no rule as to when trials should be stopped, but since additional trials can be promptly processed with high speed computers, a sufficient number should be used to obtain a good cross section of alternative districting plans.

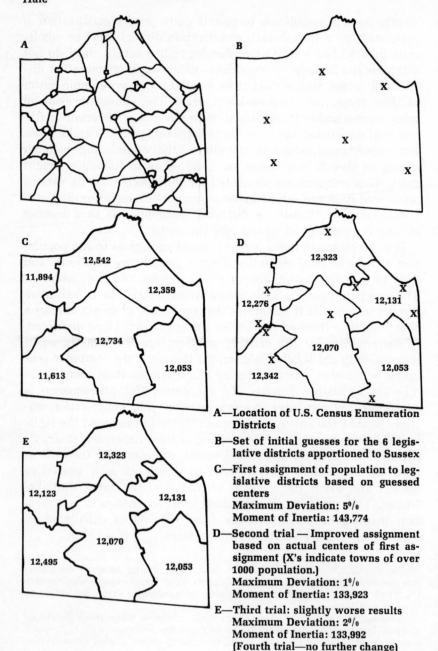

A—Location of U.S. Census Enumeration
Districts

B—Set of initial guesses for the 6 legislative districts apportioned to Sussex

C—First assignment of population to legislative districts based on guessed
centers
Maximum Deviation: 5%
Moment of Inertia: 143,774

D—Second trial — Improved assignment
based on actual centers of first assignment (X's indicate towns of over
1000 population.)
Maximum Deviation: 1%
Moment of Inertia: 133,923

E—Third trial: slightly worse results
Maximum Deviation: 2%
Moment of Inertia: 133,992
(Fourth trial—no further change)

In sum, Weaver and Hess have proposed a mathematically-based procedure for districting. It utilizes existing computer programming techniques to locate a given number of districts within a given area, by combining small areas of known population in accordance with selected criteria of representation. Two of the criteria, population and contiguity, are self-explanatory and measurable. In addition, the procedure recommended in the Weaver-Hess program introduces a quantitative measure of compactness which tends to minimize the perimeter and locate districts around population centers. By greatly reducing the number of choices that must be made, introduction of this third criterion assists in the development of an impartial districting procedure. The program could be modified to accommodate additional criteria.

The Forrest Method

Advanced by Edward Forrest, the "diminishing fractions mapping" method, which is proprietary and arbitrarily develops districts by successively dividing the areas in halves, strives to maximize population equality, disregarding all other factors. Contiguity is maintained, but not compactness. The districts are rectangular to square in shape. Marketing the technique commercially, Forrest produced districting plans for New Jersey and New York.

According to Forrest, it is possible to handle thousands of units of information, place them in geography, move them around in geography and come up with a neutral answer; an answer that adds up and has built-in proofs of having accounted for every piece of data being considered; and a process which can be duplicated precisely by anyone with access to a common IBM 1401.[9]

The method of diminishing halves is merely a computer pass played against the program wherein a master data tape for a given state is examined and broken down into diminishing fractions. When the computer has completed its pass, it has broken down the population with regard to geography into a requisite number

---

[9]See Edward Forrest, "Electronic Reapportionment Mapping," *Data Processing Magazine* (July, 1965). See also Edward Forrest, "Computerized Reapportionment Mapping of the State of New Jersey," a paper given at the ALI-ABA Conference.

of equal population districts. It does not matter how many equal population districts are requested. The computer program will deliver the groupings plus or minus one-half of one per cent in variation.

With the creation of district x-y plotting tapes, containing in digital language the assignments of population units to geography, the next step is to create electronically the map showing the district lines for an entire state on an electronic graphic recorder. That is the end of the program.

DISTRICTING BY THE "DIMINISHING HALVES" METHOD

Area: 7 equal population districts

C.

3/7 of the population   **D.**

B.

4/7 of the population   Enumeration Districts or Census Tracts

A. (starting)

If the area were to be divided into 7 equal population districts, this program provides for the first division of 4/7 of the population beginning from A. Each half would then be divided again, etc., until 7 equal population districts were obtained. The unit of population used for the program could be enumeration districts or census tracts. When the division is made, all of the population in the enumeration district or census tract is thrown to one or the other side of the line. A variety of solutions are possible depending on the starting point.

The OSU Method (Hale, Ransom, Ramsey)

This method was developed as part of a graduate seminar in political science at The Ohio State University.[10] The program

---

[10]The seminar was directed by the author. Sally Ramsey, graduate student in political science, worked with Dr. D. Ransom Whitney, Department of Mathematics, who formulated the program. See Myron Q. Hale (ed.), "Representation and Reapportionment," *Political Studies,* No. 2, Department of Political Science, Ohio State University, March, 1965.

produces districts substantially equal in population which are pie shaped—wedge districts—about a circular district centered on the population centroid. With one exception, these districts are designed to be heterogeneous in nature—combining the center city, the suburb, and rural area. Of course, in an area having a single predominating population concentration, wedge-shaped districts will have less socio-economic heterogeneity. Other plans used within a single large city tend to produce homogeneous districts. Contiguity, but not compactness, is a criterion in this method.

The method formulated at OSU differs in that it considers the districting problem in microcosm, in contrast to the other programs

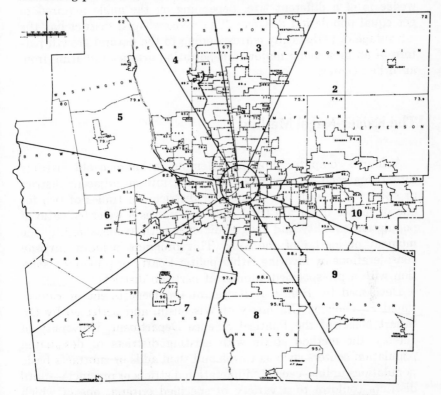

DISTRICTING FRANKLIN COUNTY BY THE OSU METHOD

Population units were developed from census tracts, rounded to the nearest 1,000 population. X and y coordinates for each population unit were plotted, assuming the entire population to be located at the center of each unit. The program is written to permit the use of actual population figures.

which were developed for the purpose of districting an entire state in a single operation. While the technique is designed specifically for use in districting in which it is desired to retain county lines insofar as possible, it is applicable to the districting of a large state having a number of centers of population concentration only when employed on a section-by-section basis.

The method locates the population center of an area and finds the radius of a circle around the population center containing the amount of population desired in one district—assuring central city representation. A ray starting from the north is rotated to the right until the sector contains the necessary population. Each wedge is of a different size, depending on the angle required to get equal population districts. The wedge-shaped district has the advantage of realistically corresponding to the natural growth pattern of an area along major transportation arteries radiating from an urban center.

The Kaiser-Nagel Method

A fourth computer program attempts to improve old districts by moving each exterior population unit into an adjacent district or swapping it with one in another district. No trades of two for one or higher order are tried. The criterion is a weighted ratio of population equality and geographic compactness measured by the moment of inertia of the area. This program includes partisan considerations by favoring either political party or provides a solution with a pre-specified number of partisan districts.[11]

Developed by Henry J. Kaiser of the Department of Educational Psychology, University of Wisconsin, and perfected by Dr. Stuart Nagel of the Political Science Department, University of Illinois, the method starts with existing districts or designated population centers such as towns and then adds or subtracts basic populations units—census enumeration districts or precincts—until districts conform to a variety of specified criteria, one of which may be population equality. This is the only computer program

---

[11]See Stuart S. Nagel, "Simplified Bipartisan Computer Redistricting," *Stanford Law Review,* Vol. 17, No. 5 (May 1965), 863-899. See also Henry J. Kaiser, "An Objective Method for Establishing Legislative Districts," a paper given at the ALI-ABA Conference.

that can start from existing districts. Other computer districting programs draw completely new districts.

The Kaiser-Nagel Method begins with an initial district plan which is determined by assigning geographic units to districts. This initial plan is fed into the processor along with demographic, geographic and political information for each unit. The program tests against a set of criteria each possible move of a unit from one district to another and then each trade of units between adjacent districts. If the plan is improved according to the criteria, then the move or trade is made permanent. Where no more useful moves or trades can be made, the results are printed out and the program is terminated.

The program enables its user to adjust the relative weight to be given to the following criteria: first, the relative equality of population among the districts; second, the contiguity and degree of compactness of the districts; and third, the impact of redistricting on the political balance of power. While the Kaiser-Nagel method can be used for many purposes, perhaps its main advantage, according to the authors, is its ability to produce districting patterns in a matter of seconds which accurately reflect whatever political value judgments are fed to the computer while simultaneously meeting the legally imposed requirements of equal population, compact, and contiguous districts.

Additional advantages of the program claimed by the authors include: the maintenance of certain political units intact, the maintenance of the status quo as much as possible, and the grouping of units into districts which meet the legal requirements and yield the desired political result. Since the grouping is accomplished either by moving one unit at a time from one district to an adjoining district or by trading on a one-for-one basis between two districts, the computer is used because the number of possible transfers is likely to enlarge the number of possible combinations.

Since the starting point is the existing districting pattern and the incumbents can readily see what effect the program will have on their districts, plus the fact that the program minimizes change because people of similar economic and social interests can be kept together, the Kaiser-Nagel Method has considerable political feasibility.[12]

---

[12]Other computer techniques could be programmed to include some of these political and social factors.

The Results of Computer Districting
Program Applications

Not only have various organizations and committees in several states submitted computer districting plans to courts as standards by which to measure legislature-drafted redistricting plans, but some state legislatures have utilized computers programs when redistricting.

Delaware: In June 1964, the Supreme Court declared existing Delaware legislative districts unconstitutional. With the Committee of 39, Weaver and Hess (CROND) used their program to prepare legislative districts for the entire State—ignoring all political boundaries such as county and city lines. Meanwhile, the legislature passed new districting legislation which was challenged in court as a gerrymandered plan which failed to achieve population equality. As a "friend of the court," Weaver and Hess testified for two days on their computer plan. The court was interested in the nonpartisan districting alternative by computer. Comparing the computer plan and the new districting by the legislature, the computer plan was substantially more compact and had no district deviating more than 5 per cent from the average population. The legislature's plan had a maximum deviation of 22 per cent.[13]

Connecticut: Recognizing the merits of computer programs for districting, a federal court appointed a "master" to prepare constitutional legislative districts, should the Connecticut legislature balk at the task for a third time. Dr. Morris S. Davis, Director of the Yale Computer Center, was at first prepared to use the Weaver-Hess program for his assignment. However, he modified the Forrest "diminishing halves" program for use, and produced a number of different state-wide districting plans which would

[13]The federal court ruled that the November election proceed under the legislature's redistricting plan. The order was appealed. One of the more interesting aspects of the Delaware case was the courtroom presentation problems. There was a lack of planning on presentation of material, according to Weaver and Hess, but communications difficulties, courtroom arrangements, the emphasis on oral testimony, the lack of copies of forty or fifty maps for all parties to the suit, and the admissibility of evidence, made for almost an impossible presentation. See James B. Weaver, "Delaware's Steps Toward Computer Districting," a paper presented at the ALI-ABA Conference.

have been submitted to the court for the selection of one of them. The computer redistricting threat probably influenced the legislature to pass a redistricting bill ten days before the court's deadline.

California: A variation of the Kaiser-Nagel method was developed for the California legislature.[14] A data processing consultant, William Below, was employed by the California legislature's Committee on Elections and Reapportionment to program the computer to draw districts based upon a variety of criteria—population variation of no more than 15 per cent, preservation of incumbents, safe party districts, and, in some areas, percentage of Negro and Mexican voters.[15]

The variation of the Kaiser-Nagel program was applied to several areas in California during the extraordinary session on reapportionment. In one instance the output of the program was adopted by the Assembly and became law. In other cases the program results influenced the final plan.[16]

Ohio: While the OSU method may have had some influence in the state's reapportionment conflict, the computer program itself was never used by the Ohio legislature. Some legislators expressed an interest in applying the program to large counties which needed subdistricting, e.g., Cuyahoga (Cleveland), Hamilton (Cincinnati), and Franklin (Columbus).

New York: As a result of various court decisions the State of New York faced an apportionment crisis. In order to reapportion by February 1, 1966, the legislature approved a bill—vetoed by the governor—for selecting a nonpartisan commission to assist in the process. Despite the governor's action, the legislative leadership went ahead with plans for a nonpartisan commission, which was

---

[14]The Kaiser-Nagel method of computer districting was developed primarily to help resolve the deadlock that led to the at-large election of the lower house of the Illinois Legislature. Their attempt to help solve the Illinois reapportionment was unsuccessful because of a variety of political decisions and inability of various decision-makers to come to some agreement regarding the number of districts per area—particularly, Chicago and its suburbs.

[15]See William Below, "The Computer as an Aid to Legislative Reapportionment," a paper presented at the ALI-ABA Conference. The most significant changes in the Kaiser-Nagel method were those in the criteria by which moves or trades were judged.

[16]The program was applied to Assembly districts in Los Angeles, Orange, San Francisco, and Santa Clara counties.

subsequently designated as the Advisory Council to the Legislature.[17]

Undertaking the assignment in November 1965, the Advisory Council was asked to produce in less than two months a comprehensive legislative reapportionment and redistricting plan for the Senate and the Assembly in time for consideration by the legislature on January 5, 1966. As the Council's *Report* indicated:

> . . . the reapportionment and redistricting assignment undertaken by the Advisory Council . . . was technically the most complex that has ever been required in New York and probably the most involved that has ever been undertaken in any state.[18]

The "professor's plan," the Council's plan eventually rejected by the Legislature, was guided by the following criteria: equal population districts, compactness and contiguity, the town and block rule, 1960 citizen population, and the size of the legislative bodies. The latter three criteria were provided for in the state constitution. The Council adhered to county lines wherever possible.

The Advisory Council decided to proceed with two plans: one by the conventional technique of "human judgment and hand technology," and another by computer technology. The plan produced by hand was submitted to the legislature and rejected.[19] Our concern here is with the computer redistricting plan.

The Council, believing that computer technology might prove a useful tool for nonpartisan districting, contracted for computer

---

[17]Obtaining three nominations from each of six university presidents in the state, the Legislative leadership selected from the eighteen names six individuals: William J. Boyd, senior associate of the National Municipal League; Arnold M. Grant, member of the New York bar; Arthur W. Macmahon, professor of government emeritus, Columbia University; Harvey C. Mansfield, professor of government, Columbia University; Robert B. McKay, associate dean and professor of Law, New York University; and Ralph A. Straetz, professor of government, New York University.

[18]*Report of Advisory Council On Reapportionment to the Legislature of the State of New York,* December 23, 1965, p. 1. See also the *Supplement Report,* January 17, 1966.

[19]Other criteria taken into account by the plan produced by hand included certain "community interests" as well as geographical or other common interests, physical and topographical barriers, arterial highways, historical identified neighborhoods, areas of heavy public usage, traffic patterns, shopping centers, centers of educational and cultural activity, and community groupings approved by experts in city planning. See *Report,* pp. 11, 12, 13.

work under the direction of Edward Forrest, author of the "diminishing factions mapping" method. Weaver and Hess of CROND were retained as advisors.[20] The Forrest computer plans proved to be completely unusable because, among other things, the population deviations in a number of districts were unacceptably large, compactness was not satisfactory to the Council, and there were a number of non-contiguities. The greatest difficulty was in obtaining data. It took too much time to secure accurate 1960 *citizen* population data for all tracted civil divisions. It became necessary, therefore, to use for computer input data based on the larger census tracts rather than data based on the smaller enumeration districts or on individual blocks. Accordingly, it was not possible to program the computer to solve the intricacies of the town and block rule, and the maps based on computer data included many unacceptable districts.

When computerizing New Jersey, Forrest had dealt with entire census tracts in the rural areas, by tracts and/or smaller units, enumeration districts, in the suburbs and cities, and in the core-city areas with population counts by city blocks. Unfortunately much of this population information was unavailable in New York, but, in addition, the state constitution required the 1960 citizen population as well as the town and block rule. Having to move entire census tracts from one district to another produced great population inequality among some districts.

But even if the necessary information had been available and the task completed, the Council found that the Forrest method is not only nonpartisan, but the "diminishing halves" program is blind. Geographical considerations are not programmed into the computer runs. For example, Central Park was cut in half with districts running east and west. (This might have been prevented by assigning population units to other areas.) Since the computer did not "recognize water," some districts were divided by inlets which produced non-contiguous districts. Part of the difficulty was that while the Forrest program can be modified to accommodate some geographic features, the minutia must be considered and programmed accordingly. This requires extensive knowledge of the

<hr>

[20]The contract called for the securing of complete data directly from the census tract and enumeration district maps, a basic plan of the entire state by Senate and Assembly districts, supplemented by at least ten plan variants under directions to be provided by the Council.

entire state. Obviously, in the New York situation there was not enough time for the Advisory Council and computer experts to agree on computer input and gather the necessary information. Despite the results, the Council recommended that computer technology should continue to be explored for subsequent redistricting.

The Transition in Districting Arrangements

Most states have acted on the Supreme Court's one man-one vote decision. While followup litigation is in progress, the probable adjustments should be in most cases relatively minor. A major concern for the future, however, is the way the states will approach the problem of redistricting and the political conflicts which will take place every ten years. Now that the federal courts have shown that they can cope with the resulting flood of litigation, the problem has shifted to the merits of alternative districting arrangements within the equal population principle.[21] Unfortunately, there is limited agreement among legislators, courts, and political scientists on the most desirable districting arrangement and procedures. A part of the answer to the problem of districting may be found by suggesting the relation of the policy-making unit to the organization of political power.

A continuing conflict in American politics has been over the policy-making unit. From the fight over federalism and states' rights to the current dispute over civil rights, the question has been the location of legal and political power.[22] Political boundaries and political decision-making units determine, in part, who has the power to make policy and who is advantaged and disadvantaged.[23] Given the relation of the district and political power in the state and nation it is not surprising that the art of gerrymandering has been highly developed.

There are, of course, several possibilities for affecting the distribution of political power by drawing district boundaries with com-

---

[21]See Paul T. David, "1 Member vs. 2, 3, 4, or 5," *National Civic Review* (Feb. 1966), 75-81.
[22]Grant McConnell, *Private Power and American Democracy* (New York: Alfred A. Knopf, Inc., 1966), p. 92.
[23]Hale, "Representation and Reapportionment," p. 7.

puters, since a multiplicity of power centers are created. The central issue is not simply a matter of whether the computer districts are equal in population; it is a question of the relation of the computer program to the organization of power in the legislature. The fact that supporters of particular policies favor a particular type of district drawn by a particular method is not merely coincidental; to a great degree, their success or failure depends on the context in which decisions are made. Given the equal-population principle, then, the immediate questions are the type of computer districts and who assumes responsibility for the application of the computer program.

Policies adhering to the maintenance of the status quo and favoring the interests of existing elites will tend to be associated with one type of district and one method of drawing boundaries. Alternatively, another type of district will be more apt to produce policies favoring change. To suggest that district influence will be persistent in legislative behavior and policy-making is not to suggest that district influence is independent of other factors, e.g., the legislator's perception of the constituency, tactics and strategies, ideology, etc.[24]

Obviously, giving effect to the principle of numerical equality in districting is no easy matter. "Political" representation based on one man-one vote may be fair and equal, but drawing lines on a map—whether by hand or computer—introduces criteria other than population equality which affect political power and policy-making. Because each of the various computer programs emphasizes value preferences, there is no escaping the fact that political judgments must be made before the utilization of any of the computer techniques becomes possible.

Political Judgments and Computer Utilization

In one form or another the idea of "community" has been one of the most recurrent political ideas in history. The literature of political science is replete with theories of representation based on the concept of the "community." It is argued that districts

---

[24]Warren E. Miller and Donald E. Stokes, "Constituency Influence in Congress," *American Political Science Review,* 57 (1963), 45-56.

should be drawn on that basis. But "community" today is used, often confusingly, with different meanings: a generic meaning indicating a merely functionally defined unit such as political community; and a specific meaning, by which "community" indicates intimacy, a special mode of relationship in which the individual really lives in community with his aggregate.[25] Using "community" in the latter sense has compelled some writers to argue that districts should conform to the concept of "neighborhood."

Paul David, a political scientist who is interested in theories of representation and computer programs in districting, envisages a political community to be like a small city, whose population is economically and socially heterogeneous by definition, with a competitive political party system, yet with an underlying unity.[26] David opts for the rule that districts of this type can probably most often be produced if it is agreed that no county shall be divided in drawing district lines until it is entitled to more than four members of one house or the other. From the rule, he suggests two situations would predominate.

On the one hand, the situation would be rural, where several counties must be combined to produce even single-member districts of appropriate population size. In such cases, David proposed the use of the Weaver-Hess computer technique, which tends to form districts around any concentration of population that may exist, while conforming to specified population ranges.

On the other hand are large metropolitan areas and the insistence upon single-member districting. To obtain competitive party districts in this situation, David suggests that the wedge-shaped district of the OSU program, which extends from the central city to the suburbs, may be the most appropriate. His idea of a political community having heterogeneity of population, internal diversity, and political debate would be satisfied.

It is true that the wedge-shaped district idea was developed with the competitive party district in mind, rather than the districts which maximize compactness. With the OSU computer program it is possible to have SMD or MMD on main arteries running from central city to county lines, utilizing the population density that

---

[25]See Giovanni Sortori, *Democratic Theory* (Detroit: Wayne State University Press, 1962).
[26]See Paul T. David, "1 Member vs. 2, 3, 4, or 5," *National Civic Review* (Feb. 1966).

usually clusters around such arteries. This would tend to produce competitive party districts and the utility of the political community as an organizing principle for settling district problems.

But, political scientists differ over the meaning of community. For some, the small unit of representation—the neighborhood—is desirable because it allows rational discussion by a homogeneous population which is reflected in cohesive behavior, since all will perceive their interest identical with the "community interest."[27] This often has led political scientists to the further suggestion that "safe" districts are in the long run desirable because of the political check which results. They argue that given a political landslide, some "pockets of safeness" provide a check—and that we should create homogeneous districts based on "the neighborhood" with "safeness" in mind. There are, after all, areas where the population is homogeneous, and almost any districting system used would likely produce "safe" districts particularly in the very rural and highly urban areas. There is little doubt but that the task of structuring districts for great metropolitan centers points up the necessity for discovery and invention on an unprecedented scale. Districts created on the basis of "the neighborhood"—so congenial to tradition and so convenient to established power systems—will probably be "safe" districts with a homogeneous population accentuating class and ethnic elements.

While the problem can be cast in terms of the desirability of representation based on "community" and the creation of homogeneous or heterogeneous districts, the choice of a computer program depends not only on the type of districting arrangement, but also on politics inside the district. It is of the greatest significance in the choice of a computer districting program to look for the location of responsibility.

The question is not whether responsibility exists, but rather responsibility to whom.[28] Given the American political party system, the answer is, to a great extent, dictated by the type of district. If it is homogeneous, the responsibility of the representative will be to a narrow, effective constituency; if it is heterogeneous, the responsibility of the representative will be to a larger,

---

[27]While not pushing the argument too far, I would maintain that this position tends to an "elitist model" rather than a "participatory model" of representative democracy.

[28]McConnell, *Private Power and American Democracy,* p. 118.

effective constituency. The heterogeneous districts will be more diverse, and the policies followed by the representatives from the two types of districts will often vary. Based on different values, two patterns will produce dissimilar results in a state legislature. And these will appear in the form of distribution of benefits and rewards to different groups.

Political Values and Computer Districting Programs

Experience with the various computer programs and the political values inherent in each of them suggests that some computer districting arrangements are more easily implemented under certain conditions than others. The Weaver-Hess program, developed with the Delaware districting problem in mind, is congenial to the districting problems of small states with a few population centers, or counties with multi-centers of population. Since part of the problem of redistricting is creating districts in large metropolitan areas, the program has limitations. The political values emphasized in the Weaver-Hess program—which wraps the districts around the population centers—are based on the idea that in a pluralistic society a legislative body should reflect its various "constituent communities." Therefore, compact, contiguous, equal population districts should be drawn to encompass one particular community, so as to reflect its interest in the legislature. The program enhances the prospect of safe, homogeneous districts based on the ideas of common interests of a community or neighborhood.

The Forrest technique, diminishing fractions mapping, has no explicit political values written into the program other than contiguity and equal population. It was a qualified success in the small state of New Jersey, but of no use in New York for a variety of reasons. Its limited usefulness, in part, is because a variety of solutions to the program are possible depending on the starting point. This may facilitate compromise in the legislature—and in this sense it may be politically feasible. However, the selection of one of the many possible solutions suggests that the choice is based on criteria not explicitly written into the program. One of the values of computer districting arrangements is that political values and judgments can be made explicit and programmed.

Perhaps, the greatest objection is that the Forrest technique sees the drawing of districts as unrelated to the rest of the political system. After all, districts are a part of the electoral system of a representative democracy, among other things.

The Kaiser-Nagel program includes the political values of the status quo and will reinforce the existing power structure, although it can be programmed to incorporate additional criteria. Since it begins with established districts and maintains the balance of power, it is politically feasible, and undoubtedly will appeal to the power structure. One significant limitation is that the program is of no value or assistance is areas where totally new districts must be created.

The OSU program is congenial to districting large metropolitan counties and regions in states with several population centers. Although not without limitations, the technique has programmed some of the values of a "participatory" model of democracy. If the main purpose of the extension of suffrage has been to increase participation in the selection of leaders, and if the purpose of elections is to select leadership, then the best computer districting system would seem to be the one which maximizes the electorate's choice of leaders. Districts are an important part of the electoral system. The policy output may depend on the quality of the leadership, but electoral competition assures the democratic character of the system.

The OSU program could be described as a computer method by which through a competitive struggle for power within the district, some representatives are chosen to lead the political system. It tends to create heterogeneous districts—hoping for competitive party rather than safe party districts by providing for contiguous, equal population districts which run from central city through suburbs to rural areas. The program starts from the center of population with a circular district which makes sure of central city representation to offset safe rural districts. Recognizing that it is generally true that the more competitive the parties the greater likelihood of high rates of participation, the program tends to produce party competition which not only affects participation by motivating interest in the outcome of elections, but also may help to increase the political freedom of the individual.

Undoubtedly, since the socio-economic patterns of population growth, urban development, and housing availability will determine the population patterns of specific areas, there is probably little choice other than safe districts in the certain areas. However, since the Weaver-Hess method tends to produce non-competitive elections in the districts and the OSU program tends to produce competitive elections in the districts, the choice between them rests on where participation and opposition are most meaningful: in the legislature among "agents" from safe districts, or in the districts with competing parties.[29]

In addition to the previously suggested values of representative democracy which the OSU program attempts to incorporate, one of the most convincing arguments for the implementation of a competitive districting computer program is the historic reliance in most states on the legislatures as the body responsible for redistricting itself. This has probably been the most compelling factor pushing toward non-competitive district elections and one-party dominance in the states. This raises the sticky question of the most appropriate districting agency.

The Machinery of Government and Computer Districting

The computer districting programs have had their most important political impact as a "tool" of the courts. In Delaware, Connecticut, and other states, the courts—exercising their responsibility as best they can with the help of *amicus curiae* and special masters —have found computer districting plans useful as bargaining tools against hesitant legislatures. Facing the possibility of computer redistricting programs, legislatures have been motivated to reach at least temporary agreement. Presumably the courts would prefer to divest themselves of much of this responsibility; but the time will not come soon under the existing doctrines of the Supreme Court unless and until there is marked improvement in the machinery of government for the routinization of reapportioning and redistricting procedures.

---

[29]One author suggests that competition should be between the two houses of the legislature with representatives from heterogeneous districts in one house and representative from homogeneous districts in the other. See Royce Hanson, *The Political Thicket* (Englewood Cliffs, New Jersey: Prentice-Hall Inc., 1965), pp. 130-131.

Apportioning and districting procedures can be established and carried out by statute, constitutional provision, or both. Reapportioning can be implemented by the state legislatures themselves, administrative commission, or the court. In each case the important issue is the degree of discretionary power given the apportioning agency. A partisan agency inherently apportions according to partisan considerations rather than objective criteria. The problem, then, is the practicality of having a legislature or a partisan apportioning board with wide discretionary powers responsible for redistricting given the political pressures and considerations involved.

The elimination of the various consequences of gerrymandering requires the establishment of automatic and impersonal procedures for carrying out reapportioning and redistricting. Given the policy process in the states, what is the most feasible and desirable method for making and implementing reapportionment policy? It is suggested that a nonpartisan commission which could make a continuing study would likely be the most useful device to facilitate the necessary adjustments. Such a commission could carry out redistricting within the established guidelines while studying and redefining the limits of malapportionment. A nonpartisan commission would provide machinery for redistricting that is wholly removed from the legislature, state-wide in its orientation, as nearly automatic as possible if based on a computer program, and subject to judicial review for inaction as well as improper action. Computer programs offer the possibility of making the task automatic if political judgments make their utilization possible. The limited choice in the districting arrangements produced by the computer methods at present does not preclude the development of other computer programs or the computerization of other "scientific" methods.[30] It does mean, however, that a nonpartisan commission interested in implementing one of the automatic computer districting programs must decide on the most desirable type of computer districting arrangement.

---

[30]See, for example, William Vickrey, "On the Prevention of Gerrymandering," *Political Science Quarterly,* LXXVI, No. 1 (March, 1961), 105-110; and Curtis C. Harris, Jr., "A Scientific Method of Districting," *Behavioral Sciences,* Vol. 9, No. 3 (July, 1964), 219-225. Limited experience with these methods suggests that they tend to create safe districts.

The argument for a nonpartisan redistricting commission recognizes that the entire problem of representation in the political system cannot be subsumed under legislative representation. There are additional channels for "political" representation, e.g., state and national executives and some courts. Indeed, there are many other kinds of representation, e.g., economic, social, religious, etc., but the channels for these types of representation are the various voluntary organizations of the pressure group system. The argument for a nonpartisan commission implementing the automatic districting arrangements of a computer program which tends to create competitive equal population legislative districts is based on the values of representative democracy. The meaning of "political" representation is that representatives are elected by the individuals in society regardless of their socio-economic status, and that each aggregation of individuals has the same number of representatives as any other. The democratic nature of the electoral system is assured by the creation of competitive districts which provide for a choice of leaders and emphasize the values of political participation and the maximization of political freedom.

chapter ten

Representation and Apportionment: the Search for a Theory

William P. Irwin

The representative function in a democracy has been a matter of discussion in America sporadically since the colonial period, reaching a periodic peak of popular interest during this century at the publication of each decennial census, when the state legislatures have acted—or failed to act—on their own reapportionment. In recent years, however, sustained attention to the problem has been generated, absorbing scholars, jurists, civic groups and somewhat more reluctantly, the legislatures themselves, in more than a decade of debate and reform. The period can probably best be dated from 1955, with the publication of Gordon Baker's *Rural Versus Urban Political Power: The Nature and Consequences of Unbalanced Representation.*[1] The importance of Baker's work was not simply that it sounded an overdue call to general quarters in the fitful conflict over apportionment, but it set the general course and limits of inquiry which have dominated the ensuing scholarly discussion.

---

[1]Gordon Baker, *Rural versus Urban Power: The Nature and Consequences of Unbalanced Representation* (Garden City, N.Y.: Doubleday & Company, Inc., 1955).

Baker's thesis is well-known and can be summarized briefly. Equality of representation as embodied in the doctrine, "one man-one vote," had for a variety of reasons been progressively disregarded as the basis of legislative apportionment in the United States since the end of the nineteenth century. Acting on a cultural distrust of urban life which certain urban-based groups found to be congenial to their interests, both the state legislatures and the United States House of Representatives had permitted or actively promoted a sharp imbalance of rural and urban representation, almost completely to the former's advantage. This condition, Baker properly concluded, posed an ethical issue for both democratic theory and practice. A highly significant aspect of Baker's presentation of 1955, one which raises a serious question about the consistency of his case, but which has been either overlooked or ignored by most subsequent writers, was his point that theories of individualism may be inadequate to the process of representation today, and that group dynamics theory may have greater utility. This question will be discussed at length below.

There is little question that the flood of studies of malapportionment since 1955 has strongly influenced the course of legislative apportionment, by acting directly upon the state legislatures and indirectly upon them through the courts. Nor is there any doubt that the historically confused problem of the "right to vote," or the right to have one's vote counted, has been somewhat clarified. But there remains a serious question of whether many recent scholarly and judicial contributions to the apportionment reform movement have not obscured the theory of representation more than they have illuminated it.

The heart of the problem lies in the highly equivocal use of the term "representation," which has had a varied and ambiguous career in the history of western political thought. A rich store of commentary on representative government, ranging from the works of classical scholars to R. A. Dahl's *Preface to Democratic Theory*,[2] is obviously pertinent and demands some attention in the current apportionment controversy. The best that can be done in this brief space, however, is to raise some of the central questions about the

---

[2]Robert A. Dahl, *A Preface to Democratic Theory* (Chicago: University of Chicago Press, 1956).

theory and process of representation which thus far have been
inadequately considered.

The Representative System

Representation may be defined as the authoritative exercise
of power on behalf of another. Ideally the relationship between
the two parties may be simple and direct, as between parent and
child, attorney and client, or legislator and individual constituent.
Or it may be complex and indirect, as it tends to be in any large
organization including the political system, in which the parties
to the relationship are many and varied and their roles overlapping,
frequently interchangeable and sometimes ambivalent.

There are two apparent reasons, however, why the instance of
simple and direct representation can be considered little more than
an analytic model, occurring "in reality," if at all, with negligible
frequency. In the first place, the relationship is continuously influenced by norms and sanctions imposed by "third parties" in the
environment, ranging from the Supreme Court to precinct chair-
men. The representative relation of the attorney to his client, for
example, is hedged about at each moment by law, ethical standards,
custom, technology, and a host of accidental forces acting from
without. Even in the most isolated circumstances it is difficult to
imagine a representative relationship operating free of material and
cultural constraints.

But this argument presents its own difficulty. To speak of
"environmental influences" upon the representative relationship
is to suggest, without psychological justification, that such forces
can in all cases be identified and considered as independent variables in the transaction, rather than as elements—perhaps even
the sum—of the perceptions of the parties involved. For practical
purposes, no further explanation is needed for the complaint that
a representative relationship has been strained or destroyed because
the legislator took a bribe. It is quite a different matter, however,
to remark that the relationship between a legislator and his
constituent (attorney and client, parent and child) has seemingly
been altered because one or the other of them follows a straight
party line, subscribes to a natural rights ethic, or suffers from an

128

Representation and Apportionment: The Search for a Theory
Irwin

Oedipus complex. It would make little sense in any of these instances to argue that forces alien to the act of representation have somehow confounded its execution. It is apparent, instead, that such cognitive "third parties" are organically present in any representative act, and that representation itself occurs according to the perceptions of the parties to the relationship. It is precisely for this second and perhaps controlling reason that the concept of simple and direct representation is of doubtful utility.

DeGrazia is correct in suggesting that "a systems approach to the study of . . . representative government is needed."[3] The role of the representative must be looked upon as a function in a complex system, in which his perception of himself, of those whom he represents, and of the system as a whole are all factors in his behavior.[4] Needless to say, the representative's perceptions of any or all of these data may differ from those of some of his constituents; and their perceptions, in turn, may vary sharply from one another. The behavior of the attorney, to take the simpler case, is influenced not simply by his client's demands, but by his perceptions of his political and social community, his professional fraternity, perhaps his family, and certainly his personal interests. In short, his behavior is influenced by his view of a variety of constituencies superimposed one upon another in a highly fluid system. In the case of the legislator, a profusion of constituent relationships is established, both formal and informal, each involving a modified perception of his role which—if they come to his attention at all—he must identify, select, weigh, accept or reject in discharging his responsibility.

---

[3]Alfred de Grazia, *Essay on Apportionment and Representative Government* (Washington, D.C.: American Enterprise Institute for Public Policy Research, 1963; also New York: Frederick A. Praeger, 1963), p. 54. de Grazia's study is unquestionably one of the most thoughtful and useful critiques of apportionment reform yet published, yet it is marred by several internal contradictions and a polemical quality which reduces its value. Maintaining quite correctly that "apportionment is only one stage of the process of representation" (p. 30), it is somewhat incongruous to insist that political equality, as expressed in the "one man-one vote" formula, is "politically and constitutionally dangerous" (p. 63).

[4]See, for example, John C. Wahlke, Heinz Eulau, William Buchanan, and LeRoy C. Ferguson, *The Legislative System: Explorations in Legislative Behavior* (New York, John Wiley & Sons, 1962); and Wahlke *et al*, "American State Legislators' Role Orientations Toward Pressure Groups," *Journal of Politics,* XXII (1960).

At what moment, or under what conditions, in the web of inter-relationships which characterizes the complex organization can it be said that any agent's exercise of power on another's behalf is "representative," that is, invested with authority rather than being arbitrary or dictatorial? Power is representative when the several parties to the relationship independently perceive the system to be legitimate which prescribes the use of power. This is the case whether or not a particular representative performs according to the expectations of some of his constituents, or any representative institution or procedure in the system is momentarily "unbalanced" or fails to simulate in a direct manner the characteristics and attitudes of the population. Otherwise, there could be no justification for incorporating into a representative system such practices as majority decision, either electoral or legislative, partisan nominations and elections, partisan organization of legislatures, legislative committee organization, and a still greater variety of administrative and judicial practices—the establishment of independent regulatory agencies, for example—each of which is itself an apportionment device designed to simplify and clarify, articulate and abridge the cacophony of popular opinion. A political party, for example, may be considered a legitimate representative agency in its own right, or simply a distortion of direct legislative representation.[5] In neither case, however, does it square with the mirror theory of legislative representation. Political parties, therefore, must find their justification in a larger representative system. The record of many party governments, including, of course, most one-party systems and several European multi-party systems, should certainly have made the point clear. Representation, therefore, is a dynamic, not static, process requiring the continuing acceptance of all—or most—involved parties to the unequal distribution of authority for agreed-upon functional purposes.

The test of whether a governmental system or any other proxy relationship is representative is thus empirical, although the demonstration must be directly related to some theory or tradition of legitimacy which influences the perceptions of the participants in the system. Inadequate attention has been given in both the literature on apportionment and the several court decisions on

---

[5]See below, p. 145, for discussion of the implications of the doctrine of responsible political parties for the theory of representation.

the subject since 1962 to the operation, as well as to the philo-sophical background, of representation in the American political system. No serious effort has been made to ascertain empirically, beyond the elementary determination of ratios of population to elected members of the legislative branch, whether other and com-pensating proxy relationships operate within the system which enlarge both the concept and practice of representation. As it is observed in greater detail below, the standard of "one man-one vote" is fundamental to democracy, quite in its own right; it has only indirect bearing on the intricate process of representation in a pluralistic system, however. Similarly, little effort has been made by the publicists of apportionment reform to determine the percep-tions of the participants in the system. While it is virtually certain that research would disclose that a portion of the American people, whether members of the Mississippi Freedom Democratic Party, the urban poor, or a random sample of the whole population, felt itself to be under-represented, perhaps even unrepresented, there isn't the slightest doubt that their judgment would turn, not in the first instance, but nearer the last, on the measure of equal legislative apportionment. Finally, and most significantly, the apportionment reform movement has failed to assay the various theories of representation which have either influenced the develop-ment, or been derived from the operation, of the American political system. It is this last point to which most of the remainder of this paper is addressed.

The Judgment of Reynolds v. Sims

Shortly after the decision in *Baker v. Carr*, in 1962, the Advisory Commission on Intergovernmental Relations published a statement of principles of apportionment. "The government of the individual states," the Commission said, "is based on the theory of repre-sentative democracy. This means that *legislative bodies must mirror the views of the citizens* within the jurisdiction."[6] Two

---

[6]*A Commission Report: Apportionment of State Legislatures* (1962). Quoted in Howard D. Hamilton, ed., *Legislative Apportionment: Key to Power* (New York: Harper & Row, Publishers, 1964), p. 121.

years later, apparently acting on the same thesis, the Supreme Court announced its decision in *Reynolds v. Sims,* which remains the leading case on legislative reapportionment. "As long as ours is a representative form of government," the Court stated, "and our legislatures are those instruments of government *elected directly by and directly representative of the people,* the right to elect legislators in a free and unimpaired fashion is a bedrock of our political system."[7] This doctrine of legislative apportionment, demanding a legislature which is the seeming miniature of a population at large, in which is mirrored the "personal, individual right to representation"[8] of each person in the population, is accepted in principle in most quarters today, even in the breach by its political opponents. It is unfortunate, indeed, that opposition to the formulation is identified almost entirely with interests which have benefited from unequal apportionment in the legislatures in past years, for the effect has been to make the issue one of policy rather than constitutional theory.[9] But the doctrine cries out for clarification. 1) Is it perfectly clear that the American tradition or any other consistent democratic tradition calls for the equal and indiscriminate representation of people alone, rather than constitutional ideals, community values, corporate or functional communities, popular majorities, or some combination of these? 2) If the constitutional tradition required it, is it operationally possible for a legislature to represent aggregate populations in direct and equal fashion without procedural or functional discrimination? 3) Is legislative representation the whole of the representative system? 4) Is "the right to vote" the equivalent of "the right to representation"? The answers to these questions relate to (1) the *norms* of representation, (2 and 3) the *process* of representation, and (4) the *law* of representation.

---

[7]377 U.S. 562.
[8]Anthony Lewis, "Legislative Apportionment and the Federal Courts, *Harvard Law Review,* LXXI (1958), p. 1072.
[9]As a matter of policy, the author wishes to be counted among the advocates of apportionment reform. To take such a position, however, is not to accept all of its conventional premises. The author was once asked by a colleague at a conference on reapportionment whether drawing attention to interest group representation in legislatures did not constitute a "behaviorist" betrayal of the responsibility of political scientists to press for reapportionment!

The Norms of Representation

The theory of representation has not been given extensive or original treatment by American scholars, although a considerable body of literature is available, much of it quite recent, which is of direct relevance to the matter at hand.[10] It is apparent that at least five theories or doctrines of representation have had some influence on the American constitutional system, although in varying degrees. Moreover, several of these doctrines, incompatible though they may be, have been incorporated into both the literature and Supreme Court decisions on reapportionment since 1955. Each doctrine, as both Gilbert and Finer have pointed out, presents, at least implicitly, two aspects: *what* is represented and *how*, i.e., "the identification and evaluation of interests, and . . . the norms and sanctions affecting (representative) behavior."[11] They may be called the traditions of idealism, rationalism, pluralism, utilitarianism, and populism.

---

[10]Charles E. Gilbert, "Operative Doctrines of Representation," *American Political Science Review,* LVII (1963), 604-618; Alfred de Grazia, *Public and Republic* (New York: Alfred A. Knopf, Inc., 1948); *Essay on Apportionment and Representative Government, op. cit.;* Samuel H. Beer, "Pressure Groups and Parties in Britain," *American Political Science Review,* L (1956), 1-23; "Representation of Interests in British Government," *American Political Science Review,* LI (1957), 613-650; *Representation of Interests in British Government* (unpublished manuscript); Glendon Schubert, *The Public Interest* (Glencoe: The Free Press, 1960); Grant McConnell, "Popular Democracy and Representative Democracy: Reflections on the Problem's Modern Setting" (unpublished paper read at a meeting of the American Political Science Association, Washington, D.C., September 5-8, 1962); Heinz Eulau *et al.,* "The Role of the Representative: Some Empirical Observations on the Theory of Edmund Burke," *American Political Science Review,* LIII (1959), 742-756; John C. Wahlke, *et al., The Legislative System, op. cit.;* "American State Legislators' Role Orientations Toward Pressure Groups," *Journal of Politics,* XXII (1960); Douglas Verney, *The Analysis of Political Systems* (Glencoe: The Free Press, 1959).

[11]Gilbert, *op. cit.,* p. 604, and Herman Finer, *Theory and Practice of Modern Government* (New York: Henry Holt & Co., revised ed., 1949), chaps. 12 and 13. The author wishes to express his substantial debt to Gilbert in these passages, although his categories of doctrines of representation have been reduced in number, simplified, and altered at points. Although Gilbert remarks that the traditions which he discerns "are primarily academic rather than popular" (605), it is not difficult to identify their influence upon the American political system.

The representative tradition of *idealism* took root in medieval constitutionalism in the twelfth and thirteenth centuries with the development of the first European parliamentary bodies.[12] Then, as now, the tradition relied on a somewhat vague idea of popular consent in which the law is considered an instrument for the welfare of the corporate public. Its most distinctive quality is its belief that the public good is a creative expression of the whole community, or of institutions displaying the will of the whole, ordaining values which transcend local and particular interests. Occasionally these ideals are stated as ethical universals valid for all humanity and found in, rather, derived from, the experience of the properly ordered community. Typically, however, they are looked upon as immanent or formative qualities of a nation, culture, or perhaps the *volk*. In Burke's words, "The virtue, spirit and essence of a [representative body] consists in its being the express image of the feelings of the nation."[13]

Limited by their stations in life, the people are not considered competent to determine or sharply influence public policy, and there is no possibility that their particular interests can be directly represented. Maximum discretion to perceive and act upon the public interest must therefore be permitted the representative, whose principal qualifications must be those of wisdom, honor, and exemplary style. Quite consistently, the idealist tradition is inhospitable to the organization and activity of political parties and other functional groups in the political process, for such partial interests, either in competition or in majority aggregates, can never arrive at the greatest good and thus are simply impositions upon the representative proceeding.

The term *rationalism* is used to describe a second tradition of representation sharply different from idealism, yet frequently and incongruously confused with it in conventional discourse. The tradition is associated with natural law doctrine and traces its

---

[12]The idealist tradition sketched here is essentially as Gilbert presents it, although it is closely related to Schubert's "idealist" theory of the public interest, Beer's "Old Tory" and, in one aspect, "Old Whig" theories of representation in Britain, and de Grazia's "traditional-organic" doctrine.

[13]Edmund Burke, "Thoughts on the Cause of the Present Discontents," *Works of the Right Honorable Edmund Burke*, revised ed., Vol. I (Boston: Little, Brown and Company, 1865-1867).

origins to the Hellenistic schools, particularly to Stoicism.[14] Its modern development stems from the Enlightenment, and it passed into American usage largely from the English experience. Unlike the collectivism of the idealist tradition, rationalism is highly individualist; indeed, in all ultimate things a person can only represent himself, for salvation is not a social undertaking, but private and outside the realm of social consent achieved according to the ethic of natural right. Far from generating or articulating the public good, therefore, it is the primary responsibility of the polity to enhance and preserve the sphere of private utilities, which are characteristically identified as natural rights, confining itself to the activities of maintaining public security and tranquillity.

What, then, is represented in the rationalist polity? It is one of the continuing dilemmas of the doctrine that, in its own terms, liberty and privacy cannot be represented, but only the secondary and instrumental needs of the citizen for justice and security. "Rational and independent, joined to others by his own free contracts, not by traditional status,"[15] the man of the rationalist tradition can never have his interests properly represented, except his interest in maintaining the obligation of the public contract. It is neither individuals nor collectivities which are represented in the rationalist tradition, therefore, but the integrity of the instruments of consent—the social contract itself, to use an old-fashioned term. The doctrine is thus roughly the equivalent of "constitutionalism," as Gilbert notes.[16]

The behavior of the representative in the rationalist tradition is troubled by the same dilemma of public versus private interest. As a rational man whose attention is absorbed first in the ethic of natural right, he requires broad discretion, free of public pressures, to discharge his responsibility. For this reason, too, and in much the same manner as the idealist, he is dismayed by the clamor of politics, preferring the reasonable discourse of his peers to the opinions of political parties, interest groups, or even popular

[14]This account does not accord entirely with Gilbert's, and draws rather heavily on Beer's description of the "Liberal" tradition of representation in Britain. Schubert presents a somewhat different rationalist theory of the public interest, not unlike the utilitarian doctrine described herein. "The Rationalists are positivists. . . They find both the ultimate and the proximate source of public-policy goals to repose in the people. . . Ideally, governmental decision-making processes become value-neutral technical processes, and the authority of public officials is the authority of expertise." Schubert, *The Public Interest,* pp. 30-31.
[15]Beer, *Representation of Interests in British Government,* p. 45.
[16]Gilbert, "Operative Doctrines of Representation," p. 609.

majorities. On the other hand, the rationalist representative is bound—it might be said "instructed"—by the same system of positive political obligations as other citizens and is expected to play the difficult and ambiguous role, therefore, of indirectly representing his constituents by directly representing and upholding their constitutional rights and obligations.

The pluralist tradition is well known to contemporary political science because of the recent intense interest, particularly in the United States, in political group behavior and group theory. As Beer makes clear, however, the career of the "interested member" is not a recent or surprising discovery, but has been given extensive justification in British constitutional experience.[17] The direct parliamentary representation of corporate interests—municipalities, universities, the church, and other major institutions—was a part of eighteenth century Whig political practice and has, of course, been revived in contemporary Commonwealth and European practice in the form of parliamentary and administrative representation of vocational groups, industrial groups, and minority national groups, in particular.

Pluralist doctrine rests on the observation that, in the more highly developed national economies, vocational specialization, education, and leisure have fostered the multiplication of organized groups clamoring for access to the machinery of public policy. The pluralist is prepared to accommodate and justify such groups as the best, perhaps the only, means of articulating the public interest. Pluralists differ among themselves on the ends of the polity. To the "pure" group theorists, following Bentley and Dewey, there are no *a priori* standards of performance for the political system; rather, both the problem of politics and its greatest achievement lies in maximizing communication and choice among the many "publics" which comprise the greater community.[18] Theoretically less rigorous, but more influential in the tradition, is a larger group of pluralists who accept and justify the group decision-making process while defending a set of political norms which are extraneous to the group process itself. The tradition is consistent, however, in its attack on "arithmetical democracy," the belief that neither discrete individuals nor undifferentiated national or local aggregates

---

[17] The pluralist tradition has been widely and uniformly described. Beer refers both to the "Old Whig" and the "functional representation" tradition in British history; Gilbert uses the term "pragmatist," Schubert, "realist," and de Grazia, "free-group" to identify the doctrine. The term "pluralist" is preferred here because of its contemporary usage in American political science.

[18] See Gilbert, *op. cit.*, p. 613.

can be represented without reference to their particular and articulated interests.

The role of the representative in the tradition is ambiguous, reflecting the differences among pluralist advocates. As the instructed deputy of a particular constituent group, the representative may be assumed to have little or no discretion in discharging his responsibilities; as the steward of a fluid parliamentary process of bargaining and negotiation among groups, perhaps a process which is understood to be limited by some external standard of value (e.g., natural rights), he may exercise broad discretion in compromising competing group interests. Because the parliamentary body itself tends to exhibit the qualities of an interest group; however, the representative is subject in any event to a conflict of roles which affords him some degree of personal discretion.

The term *utilitarianism* is used to indicate a tradition of responsible majoritarianism which has had wide academic and popular acceptance in the United States.[19] Except for one important difference, it tends to merge with the populist doctrine, described below. The tradition has its roots in the utilitarianism of Locke, Helvetius, Bentham and the two Mills, but has had its relevant development (for purposes of this account) in late nineteenth and twentieth century American politics and political science. Like the rationalist tradition, but sharply at odds with both idealist and pluralist theory, utilitarianism is firmly individualist and egalitarian; it does not, however, accept the rationalist belief in the existence of natural rights. The highest purpose of the polity, rather, is to maintain a social environment, by whatever governmental course of activity or inactivity may be indicated, conducive to individual growth and happiness.

The characteristic quality of American utilitarianism is its majoritarianism, a principle which suffered from ambivalence in the European antecedents of the tradition, particularly in the work of John Stuart Mill. For operational purposes, it is maintained, the only satisfactory measure of the greatest good is majority preference, a majority informed and mobilized by two or more (but preferably two) national political parties offering clear policy

---

[19]The author describes a tradition of utilitarianism much less complex and more central than that which Gilbert gives the same name. It is similar in many respects to Schubert's "rationalist" theory of the public interest and de Grazia's account of the "egalitarian-majoritarian" ideology.

alternatives. The responsibility of the representative is not directly to an electoral majority, but to a mandated program and to the partisan organization responsible for that program which a popular majority has endorsed. Like the idealists, who find their "mandate" in immanent community values, the utilitarians are distrustful of political interest groups whose blandishments may distract the representative from his duties. Some discretion is permitted the representative to interpret and structure the opinion of the popular majority. Yet while he is freed of the need to reflect the momentary demands of individuals and constituent groups, he may be subjected to the disciplined instructions of his political party, which is the legatee of the majority.

It is difficult to trace the antecedents of the *populist* tradition. It is related to the utilitarianism described here in much the same manner that the Oxford idealism of T. H. Green and Bernard Bosanquet was related to nineteenth century liberalism. The notable property of the tradition is its reliance upon the vaguely Romantic concept of the "popular will," a "metaphysical common interest, an entity which is more than the sum of its parts," in Schubert's words. It is by no means clear by what chemistry the "will of the people" is generated, where it resides, or by what token it is known. Fortunately, these matters are of no concern here.

It is clear, however, that the tradition relies upon the utilitarian (not rationalist) principles of equality and majority rule in its theory of representation. It breaks sharply with utilitarianism, nevertheless, in requiring the representative to render the public interest, or "popular will," directly into law without the mediation or influence of political parties or other functional groups. Characteristically, this is interpreted to mean that the representative must be responsive to a detailed and continuing "mandate" of the electorate within his district, without regard, it must be presumed, to their mixed and often contradictory interests. The representative, in short, is commissioned "to mirror the views of the citizens" without partisan or personal discretion.

There is no means of assessing the relative influence which these five (and perhaps other) traditions of representation have had upon the operation of the American political system. It is beyond dispute, however, that with the possible exception of the idealist tradition each has had a rich American experience, not only in academic discourse, but also in the works of our legislatures, the pronouncements of our chief executives, the decisions of our courts, and the testaments of our citizen organizations. James Madison is frequently cited as the author of both idealist and rationalist doctrine, not simply because of his opposition to "the spirit of party and faction," but also because of his fear of the development of a tyranny of an "overbearing majority." The stern constitutionalism of the rationalist position, more than any other, has been pronounced from the Supreme Court bench, from the opinions of John Marshall to those of Hugo Black and Earl Warren. Yet the utilitarian and pluralist persuasions of Justices Holmes, Brandeis, and Frankfurter have sharply influenced the attitudes of the courts from time to time. At the turn of the century, Theodore Roosevelt practiced his "stewardship" theory of the presidency, which was basically idealist in nature; but fifty years later, Harry Truman, the essential populist, upheld the example of a strong President by identifying with "the people" against the "special interests." Finally, no President or presidential candidate has made a more unequivocal plea for reassertion of nineteenth century rationalism than Barry Goldwater, who speaks for the independence of natural man and a contractual polity whose primary purposes are the enlargement of freedom and the preservation of order.[20]

The United States—happily—is not constitutionally committed to any of these traditions. Not only is it possible to discern different periods of history in which one or the other of them has had its day, but also the mixed nature of the United States constitution has tended to make one tradition more congenial to the outlook and behavior of the courts, another to the President, and still others to legislatures and political parties. The point to be emphasized here, however, is that much of the recent literature on legislative reapportionment, as well as most of the relevant decisions of the Supreme Court since *Baker v. Carr*, have exhibited an elementary populist orientation which, nevertheless, is frequently compromised by inadvertent reference to one or more of the other traditions. The evidence is that the apportionment reform movement leans upon a theory of representation which, while obviously an option among our political traditions, is neither adequate to the observed processes of representation nor entirely consistent within itself.

---

[20]Barry Goldwater, *The Conscience of a Conservative* (New York: Victor Publishing Co., Inc., 1960), chap. 1.

The literature on apportionment abounds in such observations as the following: "The rights of representation should be so equally and impartially distributed that the representatives should have the same views and interests with the people at large. They should think, feel, and act like them, and, in fine, should be an exact miniature of their constituents."[21] The opinion of the Advisory Commission on Intergovernmental Relations that "legislative bodies must mirror the views of the citizens" has already been cited. The position taken in both these statements is, of course, fundamentally utilitarian or populist. Taken at face value, indeed, it goes beyond the utilitarian and populist traditions by ignoring the operational necessity of majority rule at both the electoral and legislative stages of representation. The implication is that legislatures must not only be composed, but must *act* as well, in proportion to the general interests of the electorate, giving no more consideration to any interest than may be "justified by their relative numbers."[22] In deference to the majority principle, the Advisory Commission concedes that "our form of government is based on the assumption that a majority of the people elect a majority of the legislators to enact laws and develop policies that the voters have supported."[23] The statement makes no concession, however, to the fact that "our form of government" permits a popular plurality to elect a legislative majority, a popular majority to elect a disproportionately large legislative majority, conceivably an entire house, or that a legislative majority is presumed to act on behalf of the whole electorate, not just an electoral majority. The assumptions are, it seems, that persons alone must be represented in proportion to their numbers, and that the act of representation must be without discretion.

There is simply no way in which this formulation can avoid a variety of embarrassing questions which are raised in the other traditions of representation which have influenced the course of American history. What, after all, are "persons"? Unless the reference is to indistinguishable units, the theory of representation must impute some value to their existence, some interest to their activities, some varying perceptions, on their part and on that of

---

[21]Quoted in Robert Luce, *Legislative Principles* (Boston: Houghton Mifflin Company, 1930), p. 338; also in Gordon E. Baker, *State Constitutions: Reapportionment* (New York: National Municipal League, 1960), p. 3.
[22]Advisory Committee on Intergovernmental Relations, *loc. cit.*
[23]*Ibid.*

the legislator, of what those values and interests may be. If "persons" are valued and valuing things, are their values common or individual and private? If the former, is it within the discretion of the representative to articulate them? If the latter, are they exempt from legislative action, or is it the responsibility of the legislator to choose among them? If persons have interests or preferences, do their interests vary in clarity, intensity, or legitimacy? Are their interests equivocal, conflicting, or even incompatible? Do some people have interests which they cannot articulate? Is it within the discretion of the representative to ponder the clarity of interests, weigh their intensity, judge their legitimacy, resolve their incompatibility, and perhaps even impute their existence to persons who cannot speak for themselves? It is precisely such questions as these that the doctrines of idealism, rationalism, and pluralism—correctly or incorrectly, the point is not pressed—make an effort to answer.

In 1964, the Supreme Court delivered its controlling decision on legislative reapportionment in *Reynolds v. Sims*. Citing its earlier decision in *Wesberry v. Sanders*, the Court stated that "Wesberry clearly established that the fundamental principle of representative government in this country is one of equal representation for equal numbers of people . . . ."[24] It went on to observe, as noted at greater length above, that "our legislatures are those instruments of government elected directly by and directly representative of the people . . . ."[25] "Equal representation for equal numbers of people" is, of course, a straightforward utilitarian or, possibly, populist response to the question "who is to be represented?". There is no allusion to higher law or the contractual limits upon representation which are characteristics of rationalism; no suggestion of the idealists' insistence upon the importance of national or cultural values which "numbers of people" may not perceive; no reference to the observations of pluralists that representation is influenced by intensities of interests among groups. Moreover the Court did not even attempt an answer to the equally important question of *how* the representative represents—of

---

[24]377 U.S. 560-61.
[25]377 U.S. 561.

whether and in what degree he exercises personal or partisan discretion in his work.

Yet the Court has not been consistent in maintaining this position. In the Colorado decision, announced on the same day as *Reynolds v. Sims*, the Court declared that an apportionment formula which had been adopted by popular referendum was unacceptable because "an individual's constitutionally protected right to cast an equally weighted vote cannot be denied even by a vote of a majority of the State's electorate . . . ."[26] The decision may be quite proper, but it is a compromise of the responsible majoritarianism of the utilitarian tradition, or the operational majoritarianism by which the "will of the people" is approximated in the populist tradition. An electorate is itself a representative body, of course; an electoral majority is presumed to act, not simply for itself, but for the defeated minority, for those who fail to register or vote, and for the unfranchised. But the Court used another basically rationalist standard in denying the electoral majority in Colorado: the rights of persons cannot be infringed by or for the representative process, which, it is implied, must be limited to certain contractual (i.e., constitutional) undertakings. The decision, it should be made clear, is not in conflict with the Court's use of the "equal protection" clause as the basis of its decisions in Reynolds and subsequent cases. Rather, both the appeal to individual rights and to the "equal protection" clause are incompatible with the superficial populist theory of representation with which the decisions are burdened.

The Court made still another observation in the Colorado case, however, which raises further questions about the representative theories upon which it relies. Although the case concerned the constitutionality of a referred measure, adopted by the voters, which apportioned the electorate unequally for elections in one house, the Court commented at length on another defeated referendum which provided equal apportionment for both houses but maintained an existing system of multi-member House and Senate districts. "One of the most undesirable features of the existing

---

[26]*Lucas v. Forty-Fourth General Assembly,* 377 U.S. 736.

(i.e., defeated) apportionment scheme was the requirement that, in counties given more than one seat . . . , all legislators must be elected at large from the county as a whole."[27] Again, the dictum may be proper. Presented as it was in reference to a plan which provides equal apportionment, it appears, however, to have no bearing on the matter of equality of voting rights. The Court seems to have referred, rather, to the pluralist argument that constituencies —even constituencies with perfect equality in weight of vote— may vary, not just in population composition, but in the number, articulation, intensity, and compatibility of expressed values or interests as well simply by altering district lines.

While the United States seems to be moving rapidly, with the guidance of the Supreme Court and under pressure of the apportionment reform movement, toward a firmer interpretation of the citizen's right to vote, no comparable statement can (or perhaps should) be made about the clarification of our traditions of representation. Not only is there no dominant theory of representation with our experience which can be easily emphasized to the exclusion of others, but with the current exception of idealism, each continues to find its way into our literature and public law.

The Process of Representation

The fact that there are several vigorously competing traditions of representation in the United States indicates the need for a detailed analysis of the process of representation, not only in the legislative branch, but in the other official and unofficial organs of government as well. Such an investigation would not, of course, validate or invalidate any tradition in its entirety; each rests on certain normative assumptions which are beyond proof. What could be demonstrated, however, is the degree to which any of these norms are operative in the system—the degree to which they are, in fact, traditions, reflecting the behavior of any of the principals in the relationship, rather than isolated fantasies. The writer strongly suspects that the first casualty of the investigation would be the hope that legislatures can ever approximate direct and equal representation of persons in the constituencies, except in

------

[27] *Ibid.*, 731.

the *post facto* sense that persons are directly and equally subject to legislative acts, i.e., public law.[28]

If we begin by isolating the legislature as a representative agency, what is the best means of determining its "representativeness"? Several methods have been used to study legislative behavior, including analysis of roll calls, interest group access, legislative role behavior, both membership and constituent opinion, and, of course, the content of public law. It is proposed above that representation is a relationship involving the perceptions of both principals, the representative and the represented, which suggests the utility of role analysis.[29] If we further limit the study to the role of the legislator, the problem becomes one of identifying his perception of his constituency and gauging his response to it.

But at the very outset an almost imponderable question arises: what is the legislator's constituency? Assume a hypothetical state in which the weight of the popular vote is apportioned equally for members of both houses of the legislature, and in which no district is gerrymandered. A close look at any district will quickly reveal that, far from a simple and direct legislator-constituent relationship, representation takes place through a network of relationships involving a whole range of "apportionment devices," each of which creates—or is created by—another constituency. Moreover, many of these "apportionment devices" are more than the inventions of interest groups; they are fixed in law and frequently in constitutions as *deliberate means of discriminating constituencies* for the purpose of electoral or legislative decision making. For ease of identification, the legislator's varied constituencies and the devices which create them will be referred to as electoral, governmental, and functional.

The most obvious of the *electoral constituencies* are created by drawing legislative district boundaries. It is common knowledge,

---

[28]The writer further suspects that systematic analysis would reveal that the representative behavior of legislatures in the United States varies widely, ranging from a mixed pluralism and idealism (i.e., responsiveness to both large constituent interests and perceived community values) in the Congress, to increasingly pluralist and utilitarian behavior in small jurisdictions, from state legislatures to large city councils to small city councils. It would likely find, as well, that the higher courts have assumed primary responsibility for the rationalist tradition of representation, and that Theodore Roosevelt was quite right in noting the idealist requirements of the office of President.
[29]See Malcolm E. Jewell, "Political Patterns in Apportionment," *The Politics of Reapportionment* (New York: Atherton Press, 1962); Wahlke *et al., op. cit.;* and Eulau *et al., op. cit.*

of course, that districts can be gerrymandered, although remaining compact and contiguous. The relative utility of large and small districts, single- and multi-member districts, and socio-economically homogeneous or heterogeneous districts has been discussed at length. There is general (but not unanimous) agreement, for example, that large, heterogeneous, multi-member districts may give undue electoral advantage to one political party or to a dominant economic, racial or religious element of the electorate; that small, homogeneous, single-member districts tend to profit minority, partisan and socio-economic groups, but often produce narrowly interested legislators; and that mixed districts produce mixed electoral results. It has not been thoroughly debated, however, whether, in a system which weights each vote equally, such "legal gerrymandering" may be a matter of policy rather than constitutional right, perhaps to be used (as political parties are) to create working majorities or (as administrative agencies frequently are) to aid some handicapped element of the population. This question, which is one of democratic theory, is fundamental to the very meaning of representation, however it may be answered; yet it has been given less attention, for example, than the arithmetic conundrum of how to distribute votes by digital computer.

Quite apart from debate, it has not even been noted that the effect of shifting district boundaries is not simply to modify the composition of constituencies, but to alter their number and intensity according to the perceptions of the legislator. In a large, heterogeneous urbanized district, to take but one example, several hypotheses about the behavior of a representative appear tenable. Observing differences among groups in his district, he may, in effect, respond to the single "constituency" of his party or its leaders in order to avoid conflict in his own role. He may, as a result of highly conflicting pressures upon him, go a step further and assume a "plague on all your houses" attitude, adopting (in his view) the idealist role of the servant of higher community values. Or, at the opposite extreme, he may take the more common representative position of attempting to satisfy several district "constituencies" within his district simultaneously—perhaps urban and suburban, Negro and white middle class—by absorbing and compromising their differences.

Other electoral constituencies are defined by the laws and procedures of elections themselves. The effect of suffrage limitations upon the composition and orientation of constituencies is not greatly significant in elections for state legislatures, except in areas where Negroes are still effectively disfranchised.[30] Of vastly greater importance, but not often glimpsed in this light, is the effect of partisan nomination and election procedures on the process of representation. There is wide agreement among political scientists that the major American political parties are, first of all, electoral brokerage agencies, performing the necessary democratic rites of candidate selection, campaign organization and finance, and voter education and mobilization. An additional political party function, more a matter of academic debate than actual performance in the United States, is that of crystallizing informed opinion, in both the electorate and the government, around alternatives of public policy. Both functions, one actual and the other virtual, cast political parties in a direct representative role, one which, at the logical extreme of the utilitarian tradition of responsible and disciplined political parties, reduces the legislature to little more than a convenient machinery for tallying partisan strengths. Several of the traditions of representation discussed above recognize the fact, of course. The distrust among idealists, not simply of partisan groups, but of all organized interests which are presumed not to speak for prescribed community values, rests on the obvious assumption that such agencies are alternative and, to the idealist, factional organs of representation competing in—or with—the legislature. The populist tradition is even more explicit on the point; the imposition of organized constituent groups between the electorate and its lawmakers both obscures the "will of the people" and corrupts the direct representative process. Among doctrinaire populists, even political parties are no more than evil necessities, requiring fenestration by a variety of popularizing techniques, including the primary election—open and nonpartisan, if possible.

To the thoroughgoing utilitarian, who has no evidence of a "popular will" and little confidence that unorganized populations can express anything of public importance, the problem is quite the

---

[30]Limitations upon suffrage are nevertheless of major importance in defining the practicable constituencies of American city councils. Suffrage is still restricted by law at some point in the United States by age, property ownership, tax liability, citizenship, place of residence, term of residence, literacy, occupation, income, criminal record, mental competence, partisanship, and registration.

obverse, however. By what means, he asks, can gross and inarticulate populations be reduced to practicable proportions for representative purposes? The answer, of course, is through the organization of political parties, obligation to which will insulate the legislator from illusions of higher ideals or the public will, as well as the demands of particular interests. "The whole rationale of the two-party system is that it should offer alternative choices of candidates and programs to the electorate," Gordon Baker observes. "In this way the parties give meaning and purpose to public sentiment . . . In a democracy there should be a reasonably direct relationship between predominant public opinion and the power to govern."[31]

Baker's utilitarian principle is probably true and certainly appealing. Its difficulty is that it is simply incompatible with the thoroughgoing populist view of a state jurist which, in an earlier passage in his book, Baker cites as "a concise summation of the theory of equal representation." It is the judge's opinion that legislative bodies must be "fairly representative of the spirit, purpose, and will of *all* the people, *without discrimination.*"[32] Putting aside the matter of where the "spirit, purpose, and will" of the people can be apprehended, it is evident that political parties are not concerned with all the people, but with some of them, hopefully a winning coalition of them, in Riker's theory.[33] Political parties *are* discriminating agents; that is precisely their function in a democracy. They are apportionment devices of equal or greater significance than the statutory provisions which normally bear the name, dividing and uniting populations, generating and dissolving constituencies, as surely as election district lines themselves. Still more, they choose political leaders, organize political cadres, and order, select, and interpret the opinions not just of electorates, but often of legislatures as well. Each political party is itself a constituency, indeed several constituencies—its leadership, its caucus or convention, its financial supporters, its precinct workers, and its popular following, all making claims upon the legislator as "their representative."

---

[31]Baker, *Rural versus Urban Power,* p. 21.
[32]Baker, *Rural versus Urban Power,* p. 5. (Italics added)
[33]William H. Riker, *The Theory of Political Coalitions* (New Haven: Yale University Press, 1962).

The *governmental constituencies* are the organized centers of power and authority within government itself, which are fashioned by the demands of constitutions and legislative procedure. The most obvious of the constitutional constituencies is the person or office of the chief executive. It is a truism that the President, the governor, and the mayor or manager are powers to be reckoned with in the legislative process; it is no less true to say that an aggressive chief executive, together with his official spokesmen, comprise a constituency which demands the attention of legislative friends and foes alike, exacting a continuous and detailed representation. A single instance of a legislator who accedes to the pressure of a governor, despite evidence that his action will be unpopular in his home district, is sufficient to raise doubt about the meaning and utility of the mystique of "equal representation." The qualifying observation that the office of the chief executive is itself a representative organ, responsible constitutionally to all the people, is simply further evidence of a complex and fluid system of representation in which constituencies are reflected within constituencies, and offices influence other offices.

The chief executive is not the only governmental "presence" in the legislature, of course. In states in which the multiple elected executive still prevails, other officers, such as the auditor and attorney general, frequently wield extensive power in the law-making process, sometimes competing with one another and with the governor, himself, for party or popular leadership. Executive departments, the more secure departmental divisions and bureaus, independent regulatory agencies, and even such governmental jurisdictions as port and conservation authorities, occasionally lead virtually autonomous lives in the legislative process, demanding and receiving representation without the indulgence of responsible constitutional officers, let alone the electorate. Even the courts are represented in the legislature, not as active petitioners, perhaps, but as custodians of the constitutional norms and sanctions which animate and define the system.

Perhaps the least noted, but, for legislative bodies, the most important "apportionment devices" are the rules of procedure which have been universally adopted to make collegial lawmaking a practicable enterprise. Woodrow Wilson observed more than three-quarters of a century ago that legislative committees tend to be endowed with all the authority of the whole, which is to say

that they are representative agencies of representative agencies.
But Wilson was troubled by the evidence that legislative committees are too seldom directly representative of their parent
bodies and, still worse, are often dominated by one member whose
investiture is altogether questionable, not only by the legislature
but by his home constituency as well.

Wilson's early insight is but one illustration of the procedural
necessity for a legislature to apportion its responsibilities by establishing, in effect, a number of constituencies, each of which, in turn,
becomes a fragment in the legislator's perception of his role. The
individual lawmaker is simultaneously a part of a whole legislature,
a single house, one or more committees, a party caucus or conference, and both formal and informal leadership structures; each of
these is an operative constituency which the member represents
as a matter of duty, courtesy, deference, or reciprocity, even
though he may be remote from their deliberations. It is no deroga-
tion of democracy to propose that, in addition to a host of other
constituencies, a legislature also represents itself, not simply as a
self-regarding school of interests, but also as a means of ameliorat-
ing the demands of its other "outside" constituents. No procedure
has been devised in the entire organizational experience of man-
kind for a legislature to "mirror" the will or interests of its
constituents, even if the latter were without conflict and perfectly
known.

Finally, there are the *functional constituencies*, the vast array
of private and quasi-governmental organizations which are active
in the political process, typically commanding representation and
frequently supplying it. The contemporary literature on both the
theory and behavior of interest groups in the American political
system is too detailed and well known to require summarization
or to benefit from additional perspectives.

It may be observed, however, that the presence of such groups
in the representative system is not easily ignored by the advocates
of apportionment reform. Thus Baker remarks that the opponents
of reform are not alone in oversimplifying the problem of representation, for we can no longer assume "that there is a direct
connection between each 'political man' and his representative ..."

The complexity of the political process [Baker continues], especially in the twentieth century, calls for re-examination of some
of the premises underlying former theories. A realistic approach

to the problem of representation today must go beyond the termi-
nology of individualism and consider the relevance of group
dynamics in the political process . . . . If we regard society in
terms of group interests we can approach the question of majorities and minorities more meaningfully.[34]

It is difficult to discern in this and subsequent passages whether
Baker wishes representation of both majorities and minorities
simultaneously, or simply majorities. The former, which is an aim
of the populist tradition, is probably impracticable; the latter, a
utilitarian standard, is a sharp compromise of the theory of equal
representation of whole electorates, as noted above. More relevant
to Baker's point, however, is the commonplace observation that
large populations do not readily resolve themselves into majorities
and minorities without prompting. Majorities are forged by the
application of a device, the "either-or" canon, which itself can
find no justification in any but the utilitarian tradition of representation. Majorities are not represented in any system; they
sanction representation. If, as Baker suggests, we must "consider
the relevance of group dynamics in the political process," it seems
advisable to do just that, without recasting the theory in a
majoritarian mold.

Representation in the American system of government—in any
system—is an intricate process. No more than passing mention of
the other formal agencies of representation has been made in the
paragraphs above. The fiction has been honored, it might be said,
that legislatures alone satisfy the norms and procedures of representation in a democracy. Yet it is perfectly obvious that the
President, the governors, the mayors, and other elected and
appointed executives are also channels of representation; that the
courts also, by any standard in the long-standing dispute about
judicial behavior, are representative institutions, whether they
respond to popular whim or transcendent principles of justice. It
is further clear (which is another chapter in itself) that the
administrative representation of special constituencies, or "clientele
groups," is rapidly becoming a commonplace alternative to the
limited capabilities of legislatures. Recognizing that some may
not receive equal treatment under any scheme of legislative "equal
representation," administrative departments were organized in the

---

[34]Baker, *Rural versus Urban Power,* p. 57.

last century for business, agriculture, and labor; in recent decades a wide variety of statutory promotional agencies have been established, notably at the state level, for occupational interests ranging from clinical psychology to cosmetology. More recently still, administrative aid has been commissioned for the aged, the sick, the poor, and the residents of urban areas and Appalachia.

A Note on the Law of Representation

In *Reynolds v. Sims*, the Supreme Court observed: "Undeniably the Constitution of the United States protects the right of all qualified citizens to vote, in state as well as in federal elections."[35] Moreover, the Court went on to say, "one person's vote must be counted equally with those of all others in a State," and "voters cannot be classified, constitutionally, on the basis of where they live, at least with respect to voting in statewide elections."[36] The significant point of these passages is that, despite the confusing and irrelevant references to "direct representation," the Court did no more, after all, than add an additional cautious dimension to the historically ambiguous concept of the "right to vote." While only "qualified" citizens may vote, the Court maintained (apparently reserving its judgment on a long list of other suffrage limitations) the Constitution cannot permit the diminution of the right on the accidental basis of place of residence.

The Court did not formulate a doctrine of the "right to representation" or the "right of equal representation." Whether such a move was the Court's intent is difficult to discern. Before any further step is taken to identify such a right, both the Court and the proponents of apportionment reform should pause to consider whether the "right to vote" and the "right to representation" may not be both constitutionally and politically distinct things. If it is possible and desirable in a democracy to guarantee the exercise of a mode of expression—in this instance, the act of voting—it does not follow that the opinion expressed will be given consideration. Representation, like credence, cannot be guaranteed.

---

[35]377 U.S. 554.
[36]377 U.S. 560.

INDEX

Advisory Commission on Intergovernmental Relations: proposals 8-9; quoted 130; premises criticized 139

Alabama: elections at-large 19; racial districting 20; population variance 26; Tuskegee case 28; litigation 28-29

Alaska: apportionment commission 50

ALI-ABA Computer Conference: conclusions 100-101

Apportionment reform movement: premises criticized 129-131, 138-139

At-large elections: effects 18, 20; extent 19

Atypical districting systems: 40-42

Baker, Gordon: rural-urban power 125-126; on political parties 146; on interest groups 149

Baker v. Carr: effects 6, 14; population variance 26; political discrimination 31

Below, William: computer program 113

Bicameral offset: legality 26; evaluated 41-42

Blosser v. Rhodes: Ohio senate case 57-58

Boyd, William J. D.: use of computers 100

Brennan, Justice William: dictum in Dorsey case 13

British Boundary Commissions: functions 9

Buckley v. Hoff: population variance 26

Burke, Edmund: quoted 133

Burns v. Richardson: use of registered voters 30; representation of minorities 30f; use of multi-member districts 32-33

Butcher v. Bloom: balancing interests 27

California: referendum 21; use of computer 113

Cities and counties: division of 2, 44-45, 56

Colorado: referendum voided 6, 21; new districts 19; Lucas case 31, 32, 141

Communities: treatment of 10-11, 118; political community 117-120; districting to reflect 118-120

Competitive and safe districts: fostering 44-46; as criteria 74; effect on party system 80; effects and merits 118-120; computer programs 118-122

Computers: potential use of 3-4, 100; appraised 49; methods of districting 99-124; distribution of power 99, 116-117; non-partisan program 100; ALI-ABA Conference 100-101; Weaver-Hess program 100, 103-107; gerrymandering 101, 123-124; four districting programs 103-112; use in states 112-116; use by courts 112, 122; heterogeneous districts 118-120; competitive districts 118-119; appraisal of programs 120-122

Congressional districts: as legislative districts 80-81

Connecticut: constitution 21; use of computer 112-113